MINNESOTA BUCKET LIST

Set Off on **120 Epic Adventures** and Discover
Incredible Destinations to Live Out Your Dreams
While Creating Unforgettable Memories
that Will Last a Lifetime.

**(Online Digital MAP included - access it through
the link provided in the MAP Chapter of this book)**

BeCrePress Travel

MINNESOTA BUCKET LIST

table of contents

MINNESOTA BUCKET LIST

TABLE OF CONTENTS

MINNESOTA BUCKET LIST

MINNESOTA BUCKET LIST

MINNESOTA BUCKET LIST

INTRODUCTION

Welcome to Minnesota Bucket List!

Get ready to immerse yourself in the wonders of the North Star State, where every twist of the road and bend of the river uncovers a hidden gem, waiting for you to explore. T
his isn't your average travel guide—*it's your personal ticket to adventure*, a treasure map to 120 of Minnesota's most breathtaking and exciting destinations, all guaranteed to ignite your sense of wanderlust and create memories you'll cherish for a lifetime.

Are you ready to dive into a world where towering cliffs meet sparkling waters, where wildlife roams free in dense forests, and where history whispers through the winds of vast prairies?

Picture yourself standing in awe beneath the legendary Split Rock Lighthouse, marveling at the rugged beauty of the North Shore. Or perhaps you'll lose yourself in the magic of the Minneapolis Sculpture Garden, where art and nature blend seamlessly.

Whether you're exploring Minnesota's vibrant cultural scene, gazing up at the majestic Great Lakes, or hiking through pristine state parks, this book is your gateway to experiencing Minnesota's most extraordinary destinations.

Each destination in this guide is carefully curated, offering not just a place to visit, but an adventure waiting to unfold. Alongside stunning descriptions that will help you picture each spot before you even arrive, we've made sure all the details you need are at your fingertips.

You'll find the exact address, so you never have to worry about getting lost, and we've included the nearest city, so you can always orient yourself. With the GPS coordinates ready to be entered into your device, you can start your journey with confidence, knowing you'll arrive at your dream destination with ease.

But we didn't stop there! You'll also discover the best times of the year to visit each location—whether you're looking for the peak fall colors, the warmth of summer, or the snowy magic of winter. Plus, you'll get a heads-up on any tolls or access fees you might encounter, so there are no surprises along the way. For those who love a good bit of trivia, our "Did You Know?" sections offer fun facts and little-known tidbits about each destination, adding a layer of richness to your journey. To top it all off, each entry includes the official website for up-to-date information and insights.

And as if that wasn't enough, we've got a special bonus just for you: an interactive state map with all 120 destinations already loaded! Say goodbye to the hassle of juggling confusing maps or hunting for locations on your phone. With just a few taps, you'll have everything you need to plan your route, navigate with ease, and enjoy a seamless adventure across Minnesota. This map is your ultimate tool for exploring, allowing you to focus on what truly matters—soaking in the unforgettable experiences that await at every destination.

From the serene shores of Lake Bemidji to the iconic Paul Bunyan and Babe the Blue Ox, from the haunting beauty of Niagara Cave to the vibrant pulse of the Minnesota Zoo, this guide is more than a book—it's a companion on your journey to discover Minnesota like never before. Each destination, whether it's nestled in the heart of the wilderness or perched in the midst of a bustling city, holds the promise of wonder and excitement.

So, lace up your hiking boots, grab your camera, and set off on an epic adventure that will take you from one awe-inspiring corner of the state to the next. Whether you're a solo traveler seeking serenity in nature or a family eager for fun and discovery, Minnesota Bucket List is your key to unlocking the hidden treasures of this remarkable state.
The memories you make here will last long after you've returned home, etched into your heart like the peaceful ripple of a lake at sunset or the towering silhouette of pines against the northern sky.

What are you waiting for? Adventure is calling! Minnesota is ready to reveal its magic—one unforgettable destination at a time.

ABOUT MINNESOTA

To access the Digital Map, please refer to the 'Map Chapter' in this book

Landscape of Minnesota

Minnesota's landscape is a stunning tapestry of contrasts, a playground for nature lovers and adventurers alike. This northern gem is carved by ancient glaciers and shaped by flowing waters, creating a diverse terrain that mesmerizes with its natural beauty.

The state boasts more than 10,000 lakes, reflecting serene skies and vibrant sunsets, from the famous Mississippi Headwaters to the sapphire waters of Lake Bemidji. Towering forests of pine and hardwood sweep across the land, offering vibrant displays of color in the fall and lush greenery in the summer.

As you traverse Minnesota, you'll encounter rugged cliffs, such as the dramatic Palisade Head, where steep walls rise from the shores of Lake Superior, creating a breathtaking panorama of the world's largest freshwater lake.
This area offers not only a visual feast but also a sense of grandeur that sparks the imagination. Further inland, the landscape softens into rolling hills and prairies that burst with wildflowers in the warmer months, providing a picturesque backdrop for exploration.

Minnesota's waterways carve through the landscape, from cascading waterfalls like those at Minnehaha Falls to the powerful High Falls near the Canadian border, where torrents of water plunge into deep gorges. The state's rivers, including the mighty Mississippi and the majestic St. Croix, wind their way through scenic valleys and bluffs, creating opportunities for peaceful reflection or thrilling adventure.

Throughout the seasons, Minnesota's landscape transforms dramatically. In winter, snow blankets the forests and lakes, inviting visitors to embrace its frosty magic. In spring and summer, the land blooms with life, and in fall, vibrant reds, oranges, and yellows create a fiery spectacle across the forests. From the north shore of Lake Superior to the bluffs along the Mississippi, Minnesota's landscape invites you to dream, explore, and connect with the wonders of the natural world.

Flora and Fauna of Minnesota

Minnesota's flora and fauna paint a vivid portrait of nature's artistry, creating an immersive wilderness teeming with life. The state's expansive forests, stretching from the north's boreal pinewoods to the oak savannas of the prairie regions, offer shelter to an array of plant species.

The towering white pines, birches, and maples create a canopy that shifts with the seasons—from the verdant green of summer to the fiery oranges and reds of autumn, to the snow-draped elegance of winter. Beneath this majestic woodland shelter, the forest floor is alive with ferns, wildflowers, and mosses, offering bursts of color and texture, a reminder of the quiet resilience of nature.

In Minnesota's vast wetlands and prairies, tall grasses sway with the wind, punctuated by wild lupines, blazing stars, and black-eyed Susans. These wide-open spaces feel endless, a reminder of a time when the great bison herds roamed. The state's lakes and rivers edge these landscapes, bordered by delicate water lilies and wild rice, the latter a sacred plant to the Indigenous peoples of the region.

Among this abundance of flora thrives an equally impressive diversity of fauna. Minnesota is a haven for wildlife enthusiasts. You may catch a glimpse of a majestic bald eagle soaring above, its sharp eyes scanning for fish, or hear the haunting calls of loons echoing across the water. Deep within the forests, black bears roam, while the elusive gray wolf—revered and respected—stalks its prey with quiet precision. Whitetail deer are a common sight, their graceful forms often visible in the early morning mist, and in the northernmost regions, the moose, a symbol of the wild, moves with both strength and solitude.

Whether you're trekking through dense woods, paddling on a crystal-clear lake, or exploring open prairies, Minnesota's flora and fauna connect you to the state's heartbeat, a living landscape brimming with beauty and life.

Climate of Minnesota

Minnesota's climate is an enchanting display of nature's many moods, offering a symphony of seasons that add richness to every visit. In this northern land, the weather is as much a part of the experience as the state's lakes, forests, and cities. Minnesota enjoys a continental climate, meaning you'll encounter the full breadth of seasonal splendor, each transition bringing its own magic and charm.

Winter in Minnesota is a time of pristine, snow-blanketed wonder. The air is crisp, the sky often clear and bright, and the ground sparkles with frost. With temperatures plunging into the deep freeze, this is a place where the adventurous revel in the frostbitten beauty, bundling up for exhilarating winter sports and the unique joy of watching snowflakes fall against evergreens. Winter seems to transform Minnesota into a silent, white wilderness, a perfect contrast to the warmth found indoors by a crackling fire.

As winter recedes, spring awakens Minnesota with a sudden burst of life. Melting snow gives way to rivers flowing freely once again, and the landscape blooms with wildflowers and budding trees. The air becomes sweet with the scent of fresh earth, signaling the state's renewal after months of slumber. Temperatures steadily rise, and the days lengthen, setting the stage for summer's arrival.
Summer is a season of vibrancy, where the warm sun reflects off the lakes, and every corner of the state is alive with the colors of nature in full bloom.
Warm, long days are perfect for exploring, whether by foot, bike, or boat, as temperatures hover comfortably in the 70s and 80s. The scent of pine mixes with the freshness of lake breezes, creating a sensory experience unique to Minnesota's summer.

Finally, fall sweeps across Minnesota with a breathtaking display of colors. The forests ignite in fiery oranges, reds, and yellows, and the air turns brisk, filled with the earthy scent of fallen leaves. Autumn is a time of reflection, a reminder of nature's cycle as the state prepares once more for the embrace of winter. Each season in Minnesota offers its own unforgettable experience, painting the landscape with new colors, textures, and moods, inviting you to fall in love with the rhythm of the state's ever-changing climate.

History of Minnesota

Minnesota's history is a rich and compelling narrative that spans centuries, weaving together the stories of its Indigenous peoples, European explorers, fur traders, settlers, and industrial pioneers. This land, where the mighty Mississippi River begins its journey and Lake Superior crashes against the northern shore, has seen epic transformations that shaped not only the state but also the nation.

Minnesota's history reflects a diverse tapestry of cultures, innovation, and perseverance, echoing through its landscapes, landmarks, and communities.

Long before Europeans set foot on Minnesota's soil, it was the homeland of Native American tribes, including the Dakota and Ojibwe. These tribes were deeply connected to the land and water, using the state's abundant resources to sustain their way of life. The Dakota, whose name means "allies," and the Ojibwe, known as the Anishinaabe, lived in harmony with Minnesota's natural bounty— hunting, fishing, and cultivating crops such as wild rice, a sacred food that continues to be important in both culture and economy. Their intricate systems of trade, spirituality, and governance left a lasting imprint on the land and are still celebrated today in powwows, language revitalization efforts, and tribal lands that thrive throughout the state.

The first European to explore this territory was the French fur trader Pierre-Esprit Radisson in the mid-17th century. Minnesota's waterways, particularly the vast system of rivers and lakes, made it a strategic center for the fur trade, and French and British fur traders soon followed, establishing trading posts throughout the region. The fur trade fostered alliances and conflicts with the Indigenous tribes, while also bringing new goods and technologies. In 1803, the land that would become Minnesota was sold to the United States as part of the Louisiana Purchase, and its future as part of the expanding nation was sealed.

By the early 19th century, Minnesota became a focal point of westward expansion. Fort Snelling, established in 1820 at the confluence of the Mississippi and Minnesota Rivers, was one of the first U.S. military outposts in the region. It played a key role in the establishment of American authority, becoming a vital outpost for settlers and a hub for trade. Over time, it also served as a tragic site of internment for hundreds of Dakota people during the U.S.-Dakota War of 1862, a violent conflict that erupted after decades of tension between the United States government and the Dakota people over broken treaties, land, and resources.

As European settlers streamed into Minnesota throughout the 1800s, drawn by the promise of fertile land and new opportunities, the landscape began to change rapidly. Minnesota became a state in 1858, just before the Civil War. Its location along the Mississippi River and proximity to natural resources made it a key center for agriculture and industry. The construction of railroads further spurred development, connecting Minnesota to other parts of the country and allowing its products—lumber, grain, and iron ore—to flow to national and international markets.

Minneapolis and St. Paul, known as the Twin Cities, emerged as bustling centers of industry. The waterfalls at St. Anthony Falls powered the grain mills that made Minneapolis the "Flour Milling Capital of the World" in the late 19th and early 20th centuries. St. Paul, with its strategic location along the Mississippi, became a hub for trade and transportation. The milling industry attracted waves of immigrants, particularly from Scandinavia, Germany, and Ireland, contributing to the diverse cultural fabric of the state. By the turn of the century, Minnesota was thriving, with its economy firmly rooted in agriculture, lumber, and manufacturing.

Yet, Minnesota's history is not just about economic development. It is a story of social change, cultural evolution, and innovation. The state has long been a beacon of progressive politics, often leading the way in labor rights, civil rights, and education reform. In the early 20th century, the Farmer-Labor Party rose to prominence, advocating for workers' rights and the needs of small farmers, and merging with the Democratic Party in the 1940s to create the state's unique Democratic-Farmer-Labor (DFL) Party.
This commitment to social justice can still be seen in Minnesota's vibrant political scene today.
The state also played a significant role in the fight for civil rights. In the 1960s, Minnesota became a hub for movements advocating for Native American rights, including the American Indian Movement (AIM), which was founded in Minneapolis. The state's political and social landscapes have often reflected the tensions and triumphs of a nation grappling with issues of equality, freedom, and identity.
Minnesota's economy continued to evolve in the 20th century, diversifying beyond its agricultural and industrial roots. The discovery of rich iron ore deposits in the Mesabi Range transformed Minnesota into a mining powerhouse, fueling the nation's steel production. The state also became a leader in technology and medical innovation, particularly through companies like 3M and the Mayo Clinic, which

pioneered advancements in healthcare and medical research that gained international renown.

As the century progressed, Minnesota became known not only for its industry but also for its vibrant arts and culture scene. From the hauntingly beautiful music of Bob Dylan, a native of Hibbing, to the legendary Paisley Park and music of Prince, Minnesota's cultural contributions have left an indelible mark on the world. The state's commitment to the arts is evident in its numerous museums, theaters, and festivals that celebrate creativity in all its forms.

Today, Minnesota stands as a testament to resilience, diversity, and innovation. It is a state that honors its past while embracing the future, balancing natural beauty with economic progress, and maintaining a deep respect for the cultures and people who have called it home for centuries. Whether exploring the history of the Dakota and Ojibwe peoples, walking in the footsteps of fur traders and settlers, or marveling at the architectural beauty of the Twin Cities, Minnesota's history is alive and ever-present, inviting visitors to delve deeper into the stories that shaped this remarkable state.

From its indigenous roots to its role in shaping the industrial and cultural landscape of America, Minnesota's history is one of transformation, perseverance, and growth. It is a history that is not just told in textbooks but is felt in every corner of the state, from the quiet forests and vast prairies to the bustling cities along the riverbanks.

To visit Minnesota is to walk through time, where each moment in history has left its imprint on the land and its people, creating a rich and textured narrative that continues to evolve with each passing year.

How to Use this Guide

Welcome to your comprehensive guide to exploring Minnesota! This chapter is dedicated to helping you understand how to effectively use this guide and the interactive map to enhance your travel experience. Let's dive into the simple steps to navigate the book and utilize the digital tools provided, ensuring you have the best adventure possible.

Understanding the Guide's Structure

The guide features 120 of the best destinations across the beautiful state of Minnesota, thoughtfully compiled to inspire and facilitate your explorations. These destinations are divided into areas and listed alphabetically. This organization aims to simplify your search process, making it quick and intuitive to locate each destination in the book.

Using the Alphabetical Listings

Since the destination areas are arranged alphabetically, you can easily flip through the guide to find a specific place or browse areas that catch your interest. Each destination entry in the book includes essential information such as:

- A vivid description of the destination.

- The complete address and the nearest major city, giving you a quick geographical context.

- GPS coordinates for precise navigation.

- The best times to visit, helping you plan your trip according to seasonal attractions and weather.

- Details on tolls or access fees, preparing you for any costs associated with your visit.

- Fun trivia to enhance your knowledge and appreciation of each location.

- A link to the official website for up-to-date information.

To further enhance your experience and save time, you can scan these website links using apps like <u>Google Lens</u> to open them directly without the need to type them into a browser. This seamless integration allows for quicker access to the latest information and resources about each destination.

Navigating with the Interactive State Map

Your guide comes equipped with an innovative tool—an interactive map of Minnesota that integrates seamlessly with Google Maps. This digital map is pre-loaded with all 120 destinations, offering an effortless way to visualize and plan your journey across the state.

How to Use the Map:

- **Open the Interactive Map**: Start by accessing the digital map through the link provided in your guide. You can open it on any device that supports Google Maps, such as a smartphone, tablet, or computer.

- **Choose Your Starting Point:** Decide where you will begin your adventure. You might start from your current location or another specific point in Minnesota.

- **Explore Nearby Destinations:** With the map open, zoom in and out to view the destinations near your starting point. Click on any marker to see a brief description and access quick links for navigation and more details.

- **Plan Your Itinerary:** Based on the destinations close to your chosen start, you can create a personalized itinerary. You can select multiple locations to visit in a day or plan a more extended road trip through various regions.

Combining the Book and Map for Best Results

To get the most out of your adventures:

- Cross-Reference: Use the interactive map to spot destinations you are interested in and then refer back to the guidebook for detailed information and insights.

- Plan Sequentially: As you plan your route on the map, use the alphabetical listing in the book to easily gather information on each destination and organize your visits efficiently.

- Stay Updated: Regularly check the provided website links for any changes in operation hours, fees, or special events at the destinations.

By following these guidelines and utilizing both the guidebook and the interactive map, you will be well-equipped to explore Minnesota's diverse landscapes and attractions.

Whether you are seeking solitude in nature, adventure in the outdoors, or cultural experiences in urban settings, this guide will serve as your reliable companion, ensuring every adventure is memorable and every discovery is enriching. Happy travels!

ALEXANDRIA

Big Ole Viking Statue

Discover a slice of Scandinavian heritage at the Big Ole Viking Statue in Alexandria, Minnesota. Standing proudly along the Central Lakes Trail, this towering statue of a Viking warrior is an iconic symbol of the town's rich Nordic roots. Built in 1965 for the New York World's Fair, Big Ole has become a beloved landmark. Visitors can stroll the trail, snap photos, and learn about the Viking Age in Minnesota.

Location: Central Lakes Trail, Alexandria, MN 56308

Closest City or Town: Alexandria, Minnesota

How to Get There: From Alexandria, head north on Broadway St. and turn right onto 3rd Ave E. Look for the statue along the trail.

GPS Coordinates: 45.8910526° N, 95.3772903° W

Best Time to Visit: Summer, when the trail is bustling with activities.

Pass/Permit/Fees: Free

Did You Know? Big Ole is 28 feet tall and was initially built as a companion to the famous Kensington Runestone exhibit.

Website: https://www.loc.gov/item/2017702789/

Runestone Museum

Unveil the mysteries of ancient history at the Runestone Museum in Alexandria, Minnesota. This intriguing museum is home to the famous Kensington Runestone, a contentious artifact that some believe holds evidence of Norse explorers in North America before Columbus. Alongside the runestone, the museum offers exhibits on Native American culture, early pioneering, and even a full-scale replica of a Viking ship. It's a captivating exploration of Minnesota's rich and diverse heritage.

Location: 206 Broadway St, Alexandria, MN 56308-1417

Closest City or Town: Alexandria, Minnesota

How to Get There: Located on Broadway St, the museum is easily accessible from downtown Alexandria.

GPS Coordinates: 45.8902321° N, 95.3780594° W

Best Time to Visit: Year-round, with special events held during the summer.

Pass/Permit/Fees: $5-$10, varying by age group.

Did You Know? The Kensington Runestone has been the center of controversy since its discovery in 1898, with ongoing debates about its authenticity.

Website: https://runestonemuseum.org/

APPLE VALLEY

Minnesota Zoo

Encounter the wonders of wildlife at the Minnesota Zoo, located in Apple Valley. This expansive zoo is renowned for its immersive habitats that bring visitors face-to-face with animals from around the world. Trek through the tropical rainforest, traverse the Northern Trail to see moose and tigers, or take a marine adventure at Discovery Bay. The zoo's commitment to conservation and education makes it a destination for both fun and learning.

Location: 13000 Zoo Blvd, Apple Valley, MN 55124-8199

Closest City or Town: Apple Valley, Minnesota

How to Get There: Accessible via MN-77/Cedar Ave S, exit on Zoo Blvd, and follow signs to the zoo entrance.

GPS Coordinates: 44.7669876° N, 93.1950337° W

Best Time to Visit: Spring and summer, to enjoy outdoor exhibits at their best.

Pass/Permit/Fees: $11-$25, varying by age; discounts available online.

Did You Know? The Minnesota Zoo was one of the first to implement immersive habitats, changing how zoos design animal exhibits.

Website: https://www.facebook.com/mnzoo/

AUSTIN

Spam Museum and Visitor Center

Embark on a quirky and delightful journey at the Spam Museum and Visitor Center in Austin, Minnesota. This one-of-a-kind museum celebrates the history and cultural impact of Spam, the iconic canned meat product. With interactive exhibits, historical displays, and cooking demonstrations, it's a fun and unexpected adventure into America's food history.

Location: 101 3rd Ave NE, Austin, MN 55912-3442

Closest City or Town: Austin, Minnesota

How to Get There: From I-90, take exit 177, head north on Oakland Pl NE, and turn left onto 3rd Ave NE.

GPS Coordinates: 43.6693708° N, 92.9746263° W

Best Time to Visit: Open year-round, with special events in the summer.

Pass/Permit/Fees: Free

Did You Know? SPAM was first introduced by Hormel Foods in 1937 and gained widespread popularity during World War II.

Website: http://www.spam.com/museum

BEAVER BAY

Palisade Head

Immerse yourself in the rugged beauty of nature at Palisade Head, located along the North Shore of Lake Superior. This striking rock formation offers panoramic views from its 350-foot cliffs, making it a favorite destination for hikers and rock climbers. The majestic scenery and the sparkling waters below create an unforgettable experience for adventurers and nature lovers alike.

Location: 5480–5512 Highway 61, Beaver Bay, MN 55614

Closest City or Town: Beaver Bay, Minnesota

How to Get There: Accessible via Highway 61, take a turn onto the unmarked road that climbs up to the top of Palisade Head.

GPS Coordinates: 47.2558573° N, 91.3057605° W

Best Time to Visit: Late spring to early fall for the best weather and views.

Pass/Permit/Fees: Free

Did You Know? Palisade Head was formed nearly 1.1 billion years ago from volcanic activity.

Website: https://en.wikipedia.org/wiki/Palisade_Head

BEMIDJI

Lake Bemidji State Park

Find your sense of adventure at Lake Bemidji State Park, nestled in the serene beauty of northern Minnesota. From hiking through pine forests to kayaking on the crystal-clear waters of Lake Bemidji, this park offers endless outdoor recreation. Located at the northern end of the Paul Bunyan State Trail, visitors can immerse themselves in the tranquility of nature while exploring a variety of trails that wind through wetlands and woodlands. Unique features include the opportunity to spot rare bird species and an ancient bog walk.

Location: 3401 State Park Rd NE, Bemidji, MN 56601-8510

Closest City or Town: Bemidji, Minnesota

How to Get There: From US-71, take County Rd 20 east for about 4 miles to the park entrance.

GPS Coordinates: 47.5351607° N, 94.8268149° W

Best Time to Visit: Summer and fall for hiking and bird-watching; winter for snowshoeing and cross-country skiing

Pass/Permit/Fees: State park vehicle permit required

Did You Know? Lake Bemidji State Park is home to one of the few remaining tracts of virgin pine forest in Minnesota.

Website:
http://www.dnr.state.mn.us/state_parks/lake_bemidji/index.html

Paul Bunyan and Babe the Blue Ox

Step into a world of folklore and fun at Paul Bunyan and Babe the Blue Ox, iconic statues located in the heart of Bemidji, Minnesota. This quirky roadside attraction celebrates the legendary lumberjack and his faithful companion, offering a playful homage to Minnesota's logging history. Standing proudly near the shore of Lake Bemidji, kids and adults alike will be charmed by these colossal figures perfect for a memorable photo op. A must-visit for anyone interested in Americana and local legends.

Location: 300 Bemidji Ave N, Bemidji, MN 56601-3109

Closest City or Town: Bemidji, Minnesota

How to Get There: Situated on the waterfront near downtown Bemidji, easily accessible via Bemidji Ave N from US-2.

GPS Coordinates: 47.4704000° N, 94.8789590° W

Best Time to Visit: Year-round

Pass/Permit/Fees: Free

Did You Know? The original Paul Bunyan statue was built in 1937, making it one of Minnesota's oldest and most beloved roadside attractions.

Website:
https://en.wikipedia.org/wiki/Paul_Bunyan_and_Babe_the_Blue_Ox

Paul Bunyan State Trail

Embrace the great outdoors on the Paul Bunyan State Trail, a 115-mile long multi-use trail stretching through northern Minnesota. Starting from Lake Bemidji State Park, the trail winds through scenic forests, past pristine lakes, and charming small towns. Perfect for biking, hiking, and snowmobiling, it offers an immersive way to connect with nature. Unique features include interpretive panels that tell the story of Paul Bunyan, providing a blend of recreation and folklore.

Location: 3401 State Park Rd NE, Bemidji, MN 56601

Closest City or Town: Bemidji, Minnesota

How to Get There: Access the trailhead from Lake Bemidji State Park, which is accessible from County Rd 20 off US-71.

GPS Coordinates: 47.5354258° N, 94.8277060° W

Best Time to Visit: Spring, summer, and fall for hiking and biking; winter for snowmobiling

Pass/Permit/Fees: Free

Did You Know? The Paul Bunyan State Trail is one of the longest continuously paved rail-trails in the United States.

Website: https://www.paulbunyantrail.com/

BLOOMINGTON

Amazing Mirror Maze

Prepare to be dazzled and delighted at the Amazing Mirror Maze, a fun and disorienting attraction located inside the Mall of America in Bloomington, Minnesota. This kaleidoscopic maze is a labyrinth of mirrors and lights, creating an illusionary experience that will challenge your sense of direction. It's not just a maze, it's an adventure for all ages, with vibrant colors and endless reflections making it a perfect spot for family fun.

Location: 335 N Garden Mall of America, Bloomington, MN 55425-5519

Closest City or Town: Bloomington, Minnesota

How to Get There: The Mall of America is easily accessible from Interstate 494 and Highway 77. Follow signs to the North Garden area within the mall.

GPS Coordinates: 44.8407980° N, 93.2982799° W

Best Time to Visit: Year-round

Pass/Permit/Fees: Entrance fees vary; check the website for current pricing.

Did You Know? The Amazing Mirror Maze covers 2,500 square feet, making it one of the largest mirror mazes in the Midwest.

Website: http://www.mirrormazes.com/

Lego Imagination Center

Rediscover your inner child at the Lego Imagination Center, located in the bustling Mall of America in Bloomington, Minnesota. This interactive playground allows visitors to build and create with thousands of Lego bricks, inspiring creativity in children and adults alike. Featuring towering Lego sculptures, hands-on exhibits, and special themed sections, it's a vibrant world where imagination knows no bounds. A unique feature is the 34-foot-tall Lego robot, a marvel in brick engineering.

Location: 164 S Avenue Mall of America, Bloomington, MN 55425-5525

Closest City or Town: Bloomington, Minnesota

How to Get There: Situated within the Mall of America, accessible from Interstate 494 and Highway 77. Follow signs to the South Avenue area in the mall.

GPS Coordinates: 44.8407980° N, 93.2982799° W

Best Time to Visit: Year-round

Pass/Permit/Fees: Free

Did You Know? The Lego Imagination Center hosts special Lego-building events and competitions throughout the year.

Website: http://www.mallofamerica.com/directory/lego

SEA LIFE at Mall of America

Dive into an underwater adventure at SEA LIFE at Mall of America, where you can explore the wonders of aquatic life right in Bloomington, Minnesota. This fascinating aquarium allows visitors to interact with sea creatures from all over the world, from colorful stingrays to mesmerizing jellyfish. Located inside the iconic Mall of America, it offers an educational and entertaining escape for all ages.

Location: 120 E Broadway East Side Level 1, Bloomington, MN 55425-5511

Closest City or Town: Bloomington, Minnesota

How to Get There: Situated inside the Mall of America, it is easily accessible via I-494 and Hwy 77. Ample parking is available on-site.

GPS Coordinates: 44.8407980° N, 93.2982799° W

Best Time to Visit: Year-round, with weekdays being less crowded.

Pass/Permit/Fees: General admission fees vary; check the website for pricing.

Did You Know? SEA LIFE at Mall of America features a 300-foot-long Ocean Tunnel, offering a 360-degree view of marine life.

Website: http://www.visitsealife.com/minnesota

BLUE EARTH

Green Giant Statue Park

Embrace a sense of whimsy and history at the Green Giant Statue Park in Blue Earth, Minnesota. Standing at a towering 55 feet tall, the Green Giant statue has become an iconic road trip stop, symbolizing the rich agricultural heritage of the area.

Location: 1126 Green Giant Ln, Blue Earth, MN 56013

Closest City or Town: Blue Earth, Minnesota

How to Get There: Accessible via I-90, take exit 119 towards 112th St East then follow the signs to the park.

GPS Coordinates: 43.6507875° N, 94.0956758° W

Best Time to Visit: Summer months provide the best experience for visitors.

Pass/Permit/Fees: Free to visit.

Did You Know? The town of Blue Earth holds an annual Green Giant Festival celebrating local culture and community.

Website: http://www.becity.org/

CARLTON

Jay Cooke State Park

Find your sense of adventure amidst the rugged landscapes of Jay Cooke State Park, located in Carlton, Minnesota. This sprawling park beckons visitors with its dramatic waterfalls, lush forests, and the historic swinging bridge over the St. Louis River.

Location: 780 Highway 210, Carlton, MN 55718-9702

Closest City or Town: Carlton, Minnesota

How to Get There: From Duluth, take I-35 South to exit 235 for MN-210 E towards Carlton. The park entrance is clearly marked.

GPS Coordinates: 46.6523325° N, 92.3503332° W

Best Time to Visit: Spring through fall for hiking and panoramic views; winter for snowshoeing and cross-country skiing.

Pass/Permit/Fees: A state park permit is required; daily and annual options are available.

Did You Know? Jay Cooke State Park is home to the historic CCC-built swinging bridge, constructed in the 1930s.

Website:
http://www.dnr.state.mn.us/state_parks/jay_cooke/index.html

CHANHASSEN

Minnesota Landscape Arboretum

Experience the breathtaking beauty of the Minnesota Landscape Arboretum, a vibrant oasis located in Chaska, Minnesota. This 1,200-acre sanctuary offers an ever-changing tapestry of gardens, sculptures, and landscapes.

Location: 3675 Arboretum Drive Chaska, Chanhassen, MN 55317-0039

Closest City or Town: Chanhassen, Minnesota

How to Get There: From Highway 5, turn onto Arboretum Drive and follow signs to the entrance gate.

GPS Coordinates: 44.8621639° N, 93.6162667° W

Best Time to Visit: Spring and summer for vibrant blooms; fall for stunning foliage; winter for snow-covered gardens and light displays.

Pass/Permit/Fees: General admission fees apply; see website for details.

Did You Know? The Arboretum is home to over 5,000 plant species and varieties, making it a rich botanical treasure.

Website: https://arb.umn.edu/

Paisley Park

Step into the world of musical legend Prince at Paisley Park in Chanhassen, Minnesota. Once the personal sanctuary and recording studio of Prince, this museum now offers fans a behind-the-scenes look at his life and career.

Location: 7801 Audubon Rd, Chanhassen, MN 55317-8205

Closest City or Town: Chanhassen, Minnesota

How to Get There: Easily accessible off Highway 5; follow Audubon Road to Paisley Park's entrance.

GPS Coordinates: 44.8616970° N, 93.5606357° W

Best Time to Visit: Year-round, though special events and anniversaries provide enhanced experiences.

Pass/Permit/Fees: Admission fees vary by tour type; visit the website for options.

Did You Know? Paisley Park features Prince's extensive wardrobe, instruments, and other iconic memorabilia.

Website: http://www.paisleypark.com/

Duluth

Aerial Lift Bridge

Experience the marvel of engineering and panoramic views at the Aerial Lift Bridge in Duluth, Minnesota. This iconic structure is a symbol of the city's maritime heritage. The bridge raises and lowers 24 hours a day, allowing ships to pass through the Duluth-Superior Harbor. Located at Duluth's Canal Park, it offers a captivating sight, particularly at sunrise and sunset. Stroll along the shoreline, watch the mighty freighters glide by, or take photos of this historic marvel.

Location: 601 S Lake Ave, Duluth, MN 55802

Closest City or Town: Duluth, Minnesota

How to Get There: From I-35, take exit 256B and follow signs to Canal Park. The bridge is easily visible from the main thoroughfare.

GPS Coordinates: 46.7790114° N, 92.0929200° W

Best Time to Visit: Summer and fall for the best views and weather.

Pass/Permit/Fees: Free

Did You Know? The Aerial Lift Bridge was completed in 1905 and originally operated as a transporter bridge until 1930 when it was converted to the current lift design.

Website: https://www.dot.state.mn.us/historicbridges/L6116.html

Canal Park

Embrace the vibrancy and charm of Canal Park in Duluth, Minnesota. This dynamic waterfront district offers a plethora of activities and attractions, from the bustling Lakewalk to quaint shops and delicious eateries. Overlooking the picturesque Lake Superior, visitors can enjoy serene strolls, admire local art sculptures, or take a scenic lighthouse tour. It's a place where history, culture, and recreation blend seamlessly.

Location: 500 Canal Park Dr, Duluth, MN 55802

Closest City or Town: Duluth, Minnesota

How to Get There: Accessible from I-35, take exit 256B to Canal Park. Follow signs to the waterfront area.

GPS Coordinates: 46.7808271° N, 92.0929031° W

Best Time to Visit: Spring through fall for pleasant weather and bustling activities.

Pass/Permit/Fees: Free

Did You Know? Canal Park features the Lakewalk, a scenic path stretching over 7 miles along the shoreline of Lake Superior.

Website: https://duluthmn.gov/parks/parks-listing/canal-park/

Enger Park and Tower

Discover tranquility and stunning views at Enger Park and Tower in Duluth, Minnesota. This serene park, known for its beautifully landscaped gardens and iconic stone tower, offers panoramic vistas of the city and Lake Superior. Located atop Enger Hill, it provides scenic picnic spots, walking trails, and a mesmerizing Japanese Peace Bell for a touch of cultural charm.

Location: 1601 Enger Tower Drive, Duluth, MN 55806

Closest City or Town: Duluth, Minnesota

How to Get There: From I-35, take the West Duluth exit and follow signs to Skyline Parkway, then to Enger Tower Drive.

GPS Coordinates: 46.7768990° N, 92.1270010° W

Best Time to Visit: Summer and fall for the lush gardens and clear views.

Pass/Permit/Fees: Free

Did You Know? Enger Tower was dedicated by Crown Prince Olav and Crown Princess Märtha of Norway in 1939.

Website: https://duluthmn.gov/parks/parks-listing/enger-park/

Glensheen The Historic Congdon Estate

Step back in time at Glensheen, The Historic Congdon Estate, in Duluth, Minnesota. This grand mansion, perched on the shores of Lake

Superior, offers a glimpse into the opulent lifestyle of the early 20th century. Explore the 39-room mansion, tour the meticulously maintained gardens, and learn the intriguing history of the Congdon family. It's a must-see for history buffs and architecture enthusiasts.

Location: 3300 London Rd, Duluth, MN 55804-2010

Closest City or Town: Duluth, Minnesota

How to Get There: From downtown Duluth, follow London Road (MN-61) northeast for about 3 miles until you reach the estate.

GPS Coordinates: 46.8151610° N, 92.0517910° W

Best Time to Visit: Summer for garden tours and winter for holiday events.

Pass/Permit/Fees: Entrance fees vary; see website.

Did You Know? Glensheen Estate was designed by renowned architect Clarence H. Johnston Sr. and completed in 1908.

Website: http://www.glensheen.org/

Great Lakes Aquarium

Dive into the aquatic wonders at the Great Lakes Aquarium in Duluth, Minnesota. This interactive aquarium showcases the unique freshwater ecosystems of the Great Lakes region and beyond. Journey through exhibits of native fish species, marvel at the playful otters, and engage in hands-on displays that educate and entertain visitors of all ages. It's a fascinating glimpse into underwater life.

Location: 353 Harbor Dr I-35, exit 256B, Duluth, MN 55802-2639

Closest City or Town: Duluth, Minnesota

How to Get There: From I-35, take exit 256B and follow signs to the aquarium along Harbor Drive.

GPS Coordinates: 46.7866719° N, 92.1004852° W

Best Time to Visit: Year-round, with special exhibits in the summer.

Pass/Permit/Fees: Entrance fees vary; see website.

Did You Know? The Great Lakes Aquarium is one of the only aquariums in the world that focuses predominantly on freshwater exhibits.

Website: http://glaquarium.org/"

Lake Superior Art Glass

Immerse yourself in the beauty of glass art at Lake Superior Art Glass, located on the scenic waterfront of Duluth, Minnesota. Marvel at the intricate creations and the skill of artists at work, shaping molten glass into mesmerizing pieces. You can even try your hand at a glassblowing class, making it a unique and interactive experience. This gallery and studio offer a breathtaking view of Lake Superior, making it a perfect spot to appreciate art and nature.

Location: 357 Canal Park Dr, Duluth, MN 55802-2313

Closest City or Town: Duluth, Minnesota

How to Get There: Easily accessible via Interstate 35, take the Lake Ave exit and follow signs to Canal Park.

GPS Coordinates: 46.7827824° N, 92.0943815° W

Best Time to Visit: Year-round, with spring and summer offering pleasant weather for exploring nearby attractions.

Pass/Permit/Fees: Free admission; charges apply for classes and events.

Did You Know? Lake Superior Art Glass offers seasonal glassblowing experiences, where you can create your own ornaments and keepsakes.

Website: https://lakesuperiorartglass.com/

Lake Superior Maritime Visitor Center

Discover the fascinating maritime history of the Great Lakes at the Lake Superior Maritime Visitor Center in Duluth, Minnesota. Located on the bustling Duluth Harbor, this museum offers a glimpse into the past with exhibits featuring shipwrecks, lighthouses, and the rich history of shipping on Lake Superior. Experience the thrill of watching massive freighters navigate the canal from the Center's viewing platform.

Location: 525 S. Lake Ave Suite 209, Duluth, MN 55802-3102

Closest City or Town: Duluth, Minnesota

How to Get There: Conveniently located near the Canal Park area, accessible from Interstate 35, take the Lake Ave exit.

GPS Coordinates: 46.7798470° N, 92.0924640° W

Best Time to Visit: Summer and fall, when shipping activity is at its peak.

Pass/Permit/Fees: Free

Did You Know? The visitor center features a working model of the Aerial Lift Bridge and offers daily demonstrations.

Website: http://www.lsmma.com/

Lake Superior Railroad Museum

Step back in time at the Lake Superior Railroad Museum in Duluth, Minnesota. Housed in the historic Union Depot, this museum boasts an impressive collection of vintage locomotives, rolling stock, and railroad memorabilia. Explore beautifully restored trains and interactive exhibits that unveil the golden age of railroading. A must-visit for history buffs and train enthusiasts alike.

Location: 506 W Michigan St, Duluth, MN 55802-1517

Closest City or Town: Duluth, Minnesota

How to Get There: Located in downtown Duluth, easily accessible via Interstate 35, exit at W Michigan St.

GPS Coordinates: 46.7810639° N, 92.1041611° W

Best Time to Visit: Year-round, with family-friendly events throughout the year.

Pass/Permit/Fees: Admission fees vary; see website for details.

Did You Know? The museum offers seasonal train rides along the scenic North Shore.

Website: https://www.facebook.com/lakesuperiorrailroadmuseum/

Lake Superior Zoo

Explore the wonders of wildlife at the Lake Superior Zoo, nestled in the city of Duluth, Minnesota. This family-friendly destination features a diverse array of animals from around the world, interactive exhibits, and beautiful natural habitats. Whether you're watching big cats prowl or feeding farm animals, there is something for everyone to enjoy.

Location: 7210 Fremont St, Duluth, MN 55807-1854

Closest City or Town: Duluth, Minnesota

How to Get There: Accessible via Interstate 35, take the Grand Avenue exit and follow signs to the zoo.

GPS Coordinates: 46.7257980° N, 92.1904940° W

Best Time to Visit: Spring to fall for the best outdoor experience; winter for unique seasonal exhibits.

Pass/Permit/Fees: Admission fees vary by age group; discounts available for members and groups.

Did You Know? Lake Superior Zoo has a special Zoo Train for kids, making for an engaging and educational ride through the zoo grounds.

Website: http://www.lszooduluth.org/

Lakewalk

Experience the scenic beauty of Duluth's Lakewalk, an urban trail that meanders along the stunning shores of Lake Superior. This popular pathway is perfect for walking, jogging, biking, or simply taking in the breathtaking views of the lake and surrounding landscape. Along the way, you'll find parks, public art displays, and places to sit and enjoy the maritime atmosphere.

Location: 200 Lake Pl Dr, Duluth, MN 55802

Closest City or Town: Duluth, Minnesota

How to Get There: Access the Lakewalk from various points along Canal Park, with parking available near the entry points.

GPS Coordinates: 46.7863214° N, 92.0951302° W

Best Time to Visit: Spring through fall for the best weather and views.

Pass/Permit/Fees: Free

Did You Know? The Lakewalk connects several of Duluth's key attractions, including Canal Park, Fitger's Brewery Complex, and Leif Erickson Park.

Website: http://www.duluthmn.gov/parks/bayfront-festival-park/lakewalk"

Leif Erickson Park

Discover the rich history and stunning natural beauty at Leif Erickson Park, located in Duluth, Minnesota. Named after the famous Norse explorer, this park offers a serene escape with beautiful gardens, a picturesque gazebo, and breathtaking views of Lake Superior. It's a perfect spot for a leisurely walk, a picnic, or simply to soak in the scenic surroundings.

Location: 1301 London Road, Duluth, MN 55805-2424

Closest City or Town: Duluth, Minnesota

How to Get There: From I-35, take exit 256B for London Road. The park is located along the lake on London Road.

GPS Coordinates: 46.7960171° N, 92.0829666° W

Best Time to Visit: Spring and summer for the fully bloomed gardens.

Pass/Permit/Fees: Free

Did You Know? The park features a replica of the ship "Snorri" used by explorer Leif Erickson.

Website: http://www.duluthmn.gov/parks/parks-listing/leif-erikson-park/

Minnesota's North Shore Scenic Drive

Experience the awe-inspiring landscapes on Minnesota's North Shore Scenic Drive, a 154-mile route starting in Duluth. This drive offers panoramic views of Lake Superior, rugged cliffs, and quaint towns—perfect for a memorable road trip. Explore state parks, waterfalls, and lighthouses along the way.

Location: 310 Canal Park Dr, Duluth, MN 55802

Closest City or Town: Duluth, Minnesota

How to Get There: Begin at Canal Park Drive in Duluth and follow Highway 61 north along the Lake Superior shoreline.

GPS Coordinates: 46.7841802° N, 92.0932824° W

Best Time to Visit: Fall for the vibrant foliage; summer for pleasant weather.

Pass/Permit/Fees: Free

Did You Know? The drive features several historic sites, including the Split Rock Lighthouse.

Website: http://www.fhwa.dot.gov/byways/byways/11185

Park Point

Find a slice of paradise at Park Point, a slender sandbar stretching 7 miles into Lake Superior from Duluth. Perfect for beach activities, birdwatching, and kayaking, this scenic area is ideal for family outings and nature lovers.

Location: 45th St & Minnesota Ave., Duluth, MN 55805

Closest City or Town: Duluth, Minnesota

How to Get There: Cross the Aerial Lift Bridge on Canal Park Drive, then continue straight onto Minnesota Ave.

GPS Coordinates: 46.7494937° N, 92.0704983° W

Best Time to Visit: Summer for beach activities and water sports.

Pass/Permit/Fees: Free

Did You Know? Park Point is one of the longest freshwater sandbars in the world.

Website: http://www.duluthmn.gov/parks/parks-listing/park-point

S.S. William A. Irvin Ore Boat Museum

Board the S.S. William A. Irvin Ore Boat Museum in Duluth for a fascinating journey into maritime history. This retired Great Lakes freighter now serves as a museum, offering guided tours that reveal the ship's operational history, living quarters, and cargo holds.

Location: 350 Harbor Drive, Duluth, MN 55802-2600

Closest City or Town: Duluth, Minnesota

How to Get There: Located in the Duluth Entertainment Convention Center (DECC), accessible via I-35 to Lake Ave.

GPS Coordinates: 46.7827790° N, 92.0972228° W

Best Time to Visit: Summer and early fall for optimal tour conditions.

Pass/Permit/Fees: Admission fees vary; check the website for details.

Did You Know? The S.S. William A. Irvin was launched in 1938 and served the U.S. Steel Corporation until 1978.

Website: https://decc.org/william-a-irvin/

Skyline Parkway

Embark on a scenic drive along Skyline Parkway, an awe-inspiring route that winds through Duluth, Minnesota. This historic parkway offers breathtaking panoramic views of Lake Superior, the St. Louis River, and the cityscape of Duluth. Take in the stunning landscapes as you navigate through wooded hills and overlooks, providing perfect photo opportunities. The unique feature of Skyline Parkway is its historic significance and well-preserved natural beauty, making it a must-visit for travelers seeking scenic serenity.

Location: RXRR+49 Duluth, Minnesota

Closest City or Town: Duluth, Minnesota

How to Get There: Access the parkway from downtown Duluth by heading west on W Superior St, then following signs to the Skyline Parkway entrance.

GPS Coordinates: 47.5232596° N, 92.5365713° W

Best Time to Visit: Spring through fall for the best scenic views and vibrant foliage

Pass/Permit/Fees: Free

Did You Know? Skyline Parkway is a designated scenic byway that stretches over 25 miles through Duluth, offering some of the best viewpoints in the city.

Website: http://www.superiortrails.com/duluth-skyline.html

Spirit Mountain Recreation Area

Thrill-seekers and outdoor enthusiasts will love Spirit Mountain Recreation Area in Duluth. This all-season destination offers skiing, snowboarding, and tubing in winter, and mountain biking, zip-lining, and scenic chairlift rides in summer. The adventure never stops.

Location: 9500 Spirit Mountain Place, Duluth, MN 55810-2098

Closest City or Town: Duluth, Minnesota

How to Get There: Accessible from I-35, take exit 249 onto Spirit Mountain Place.

GPS Coordinates: 46.7182684° N, 92.2167365° W

Best Time to Visit: Winter for snow sports; summer for biking and zip-lining.

Pass/Permit/Fees: Fees vary by activity; check the website for pricing.

Did You Know? Spirit Mountain features year-round opportunities, including a thrilling alpine coaster.

Website: http://www.spiritmt.com/

The St. Louis County Depot

Embark on a journey of discovery at The St. Louis County Depot in Duluth, Minnesota. This multifunctional facility is a haven of history, culture, and art, featuring several museums under one roof, including the Lake Superior Railroad Museum and the Duluth Art Institute. Visitors can explore exhibits ranging from vintage locomotives to contemporary art while soaking in the Depot's rich architectural heritage. A captivating fusion of the arts and history awaits!

Location: 506 W Michigan St, Duluth, MN 55802-1517

Closest City or Town: Duluth, Minnesota

How to Get There: Conveniently located in downtown Duluth, accessible via Interstate 35. Use the exit for W Michigan St.

GPS Coordinates: 46.7811000° N, 92.1039528° W

Best Time to Visit: Year-round, with various seasonal exhibitions and events.

Pass/Permit/Fees: Entrance fees vary by museum; check the website for details.

Did You Know? The Depot served as Duluth's main train station from 1892 until 1969.

Website: https://www.facebook.com/StLouisCountyDepot/

DULUTH

Centennial Lakes Park

Rediscover leisurely charm at Centennial Lakes Park in Edina, Minnesota. Sprawling over 24 acres, this urban oasis offers paddle boating on serene lakes, mini-golf, and idyllic walking paths lined with sculptures and lush gardens. Winter turns the park into a winter wonderland with ice skating. A day here is perfect for family fun or romantic strolls, ensuring relaxation amidst nature's beauty.

Location: 7499 France Ave S, Edina, MN 55435-4702

Closest City or Town: Edina, Minnesota

How to Get There: Easily accessible via Highway 62 or Interstate 494. Follow signs to France Ave S.

GPS Coordinates: 44.8668775° N, 93.3272869° W

Best Time to Visit: Spring through fall for boating and walking; winter for ice-skating.

Pass/Permit/Fees: Free to enter; fees for boat rentals and mini-golf.

Did You Know? The park's winter ice skating trails cover 10 acres and wind through picturesque scenery.

Website: http://edinamn.gov/index.php

ELY

Chilly Dogs Sled Dog Trips

Feel the wind in your face and the thrill of the wilderness on a Chilly Dogs Sled Dog Trip in Ely, Minnesota. This exhilarating adventure lets you mush your own team of sled dogs through pristine snow-covered landscapes. Experience the bond with your canine team as you navigate trails framed by pine forests and frozen lakes. It's an unforgettable immersion into Minnesota's winter wonderland.

Location: 1557 Esterberg Rd, Ely, MN 55731-8203

Closest City or Town: Ely, Minnesota

How to Get There: From Ely, head west on Hwy 169 to Winton Rd, then follow signs to Esterberg Rd.

GPS Coordinates: 47.8397916° N, 91.8546939° W

Best Time to Visit: Winter, for the best sledding conditions.

Pass/Permit/Fees: Fees vary by trip package.

Did You Know? Chilly Dogs offers Sled Dog Adventures ranging from a few hours to multiday expeditions.

Website: http://www.elydogsledtrips.com/

Dorothy Molter Museum

Step back into the wilderness at the Dorothy Molter Museum in Ely, Minnesota. Dedicated to the legacy of the "Root Beer Lady," this museum includes her original cabins preserved on the island where she lived for over 56 years. Learn about her remarkable self-sufficiency and contribution to Northwoods history while sampling some of her famous root beer.

Location: 2002 E Sheridan St, Ely, MN 55731-1934

Closest City or Town: Ely, Minnesota

How to Get There: Located on E Sheridan St (Hwy 169), a short drive from downtown Ely.

GPS Coordinates: 47.9027908° N, 91.8337445° W

Best Time to Visit: Summer and fall for the best cabin tours and museum activities.

Pass/Permit/Fees: Entrance fees apply; discounts for children and seniors.

Did You Know? Dorothy Molter lived in the Boundary Waters Canoe Area Wilderness for most of her life, earning her the nickname The Root Beer Lady.

Website: https://www.rootbeerlady.com/

International Wolf Center

Unleash your curiosity at the International Wolf Center in Ely, Minnesota. This world-class educational center offers a unique, close-up look at wolves, exploring their biology, behavior, and the role they play in the ecosystem. Interactive exhibits, live ambassador wolves, and exciting programs provide deep insights into these magnificent creatures. It's a must-visit for wildlife enthusiasts and curious minds alike.

Location: 1396 Highway 169, Ely, MN 55731-8129

Closest City or Town: Ely, Minnesota

How to Get There: Situated just outside Ely on Highway 169, easily accessible from town.

GPS Coordinates: 47.9058528° N, 91.8277505° W

Best Time to Visit: Year-round, with unique seasonal programs.

Pass/Permit/Fees: Admission fees apply; family and group rates available.

Did You Know? The center's wolf pack includes wolves raised in captivity who serve as ambassador animals to educate the public.

Website: http://www.wolf.org/

Kawishiwi Falls Trail

Venture into the lush wilderness at Kawishiwi Falls Trail, an enchanting hiking destination in Ely, Minnesota. This serene trail winds through a forested area, leading to the breathtaking Kawishiwi Falls. Enjoy the tranquil sounds of water cascading over rocks as you hike the well-maintained path. The 1.5-mile round trip offers a peaceful retreat into nature, perfect for bird-watching, photography, and simply soaking in the beauty.

Location: 444 Fernberg Rd, Ely, MN 55731

Closest City or Town: Ely, Minnesota

How to Get There: From Ely, head east on Fernberg Rd (County Rd 18) for about 4 miles. The trailhead is well-marked with a parking area.

GPS Coordinates: 47.9326837° N, 91.7556338° W

Best Time to Visit: Spring through fall for the best hiking conditions and views.

Pass/Permit/Fees: Free

Did You Know? The name Kawishiwi is an Ojibwe word meaning river full of beavers.

Website: http://www.ely.org/things-to-do/hiking

North American Bear Center

Discover the world of black bears at the North American Bear Center in Ely, Minnesota. This educational facility offers immersive exhibits and live bear viewing. Learn about bear behavior, biology, and conservation efforts through interactive displays and guided tours. With knowledgeable staff and engaging presentations, the center provides a unique opportunity to see bears up close in a safe environment.

Location: 1926 Highway 169, Ely, MN 55731-8130

Closest City or Town: Ely, Minnesota

How to Get There: Located off Highway 169, about 1.5 miles west of Ely. Look for the well-marked entrance sign.

GPS Coordinates: 47.8986481° N, 91.8875451° W

Best Time to Visit: Summer and early fall for active bear viewing.

Pass/Permit/Fees: Admission fees vary; see website.

Did You Know? The center is home to several resident bears, including Ted, the largest bear in the center's history.

Website: http://www.bear.org/

GRAND MARAIS

Chik-Wauk Museum and Nature Center

Dive into the rich history of the Gunflint Trail at Chik-Wauk Museum and Nature Center in Grand Marais, Minnesota. Situated in a historic lodge, the museum offers engaging exhibits on area history, flora, and fauna. Wander through scenic nature trails, and participate in educational programs designed for all ages. The center is a hub for understanding the vibrant ecosystem and cultural heritage of the Northwoods.

Location: 28 Moose Pond Dr, Grand Marais, MN 55604-2058

Closest City or Town: Grand Marais, Minnesota

How to Get There: Travel north on the Gunflint Trail from Grand Marais for approximately 55 miles, then follow the signs to Moose Pond Dr.

GPS Coordinates: 48.1652665° N, 90.8809511° W

Best Time to Visit: Summer for full access to exhibits and trails.

Pass/Permit/Fees: Admission fees apply; check the website for details.

Did You Know? The Chik-Wauk site was once a summer resort dating back to the 1930s.

Website: https://www.facebook.com/chikwauk/

Grand Portage State Forest

Immerse yourself in the rugged beauty of Grand Portage State Forest, a vast expanse of wilderness near Grand Marais, Minnesota. Explore an array of recreational activities, from hiking and fishing to snowmobiling and camping. This forest offers pristine lakes, dramatic cliffs, and dense woodland—a paradise for outdoor enthusiasts seeking solitude and adventure.

Location: W2MJ+PC Hovland, Grand Marais, Minnesota

Closest City or Town: Grand Marais, Minnesota

How to Get There: Accessible via Highway 61, then north on County Road 89.

GPS Coordinates: 47.9351665° N, 89.9431483° W

Best Time to Visit: Spring through fall for hiking and camping; winter for snow sports.

Pass/Permit/Fees: Free

Did You Know? Grand Portage State Forest is home to the highest waterfall in Minnesota, High Falls, which plunges 120 feet.

Website:
http://www.dnr.state.mn.us/state_forests/sft00023/index.html

Judge C.R. Magney State Park

Dive into the rugged beauty of Judge C.R. Magney State Park in Grand Marais, Minnesota. Known for its mysterious Devil's Kettle waterfall, where half the Brule River disappears into a pothole, this park offers stunning natural scenes, hiking trails, and picnic spots. A favorite among hikers, the park's landscape features dense forests, rocky cliffs, and pristine streams.

Location: 4051 E Highway 61, Grand Marais, MN 55604-2150

Closest City or Town: Grand Marais, Minnesota

How to Get There: Follow Highway 61 north from Grand Marais for about 14 miles. The park entrance is well-marked.

GPS Coordinates: 47.8180794° N, 90.0531098° W

Best Time to Visit: Late spring through early fall for hiking and waterfall viewing.

Pass/Permit/Fees: State park vehicle permit required.

Did You Know? The Devil's Kettle waterfall remains a geological mystery, with scientists still unsure where the water flows after disappearing into the rocks.

Website:
http://www.dnr.state.mn.us/state_parks/judge_cr_magney/index.html

Sivertson Gallery

Discover a world of artistic wonders at Sivertson Gallery, nestled in the heart of Grand Marais, Minnesota. This eclectic gallery showcases an array of artworks that capture the spirit and beauty of the North Shore. From captivating paintings to stunning sculptures, visitors will find a wealth of creative expressions from local and regional artists. Located just steps from the picturesque Lake Superior, it's a haven for art enthusiasts and nature lovers alike.

Location: 14 W Wisconsin St, Grand Marais, MN 55604-5017

Closest City or Town: Grand Marais, Minnesota

How to Get There: The gallery is easily accessible from State Highway 61, right in downtown Grand Marais.

GPS Coordinates: 47.7491224° N, 90.3339949° W

Best Time to Visit: Spring through fall for the best weather and local festivals

Pass/Permit/Fees: Free

Did You Know? Sivertson Gallery was founded in 1980 and has become a cornerstone of the Grand Marais art scene.

Website: https://sivertson.com/

Grand Portage National Monument

Unearth the rich history of fur trading at the Grand Portage National Monument. Located in Grand Portage, Minnesota, this historical site re-creates a once-thriving 18th-century fur trade depot. Engage in hands-on exhibits, explore reconstructed buildings, and immerse yourself in the tales of voyageurs and Native American Ojibwe tribes. Perched along the shores of Lake Superior, it's a captivating journey back in time.

Location: 170 Mile Creek Rd, Grand Portage, MN 55605-3012

Closest City or Town: Grand Portage, Minnesota

How to Get There: Follow State Highway 61 north and look for signs marking the entrance to the monument.

GPS Coordinates: 47.9624157° N, 89.6848186° W

Best Time to Visit: Summer and fall for living history demonstrations

Pass/Permit/Fees: Free

Did You Know? The Grand Portage Depot was a key trading post for the North West Company in the late 1700s.

Website: https://www.nps.gov/grpo/planyourvisit/directions.htm

Grand Portage State Park

Embrace the untamed beauty of Grand Portage State Park in Grand Portage, Minnesota. This park boasts the stunning High Falls, the tallest waterfall in Minnesota, plunging 120 feet into the Pigeon River. It's an ideal spot for hiking, picnicking, and breathtaking views. Located near the Canadian border, it offers a serene escape into nature's grandeur.

Location: 9393 E, Mn-61, Grand Portage, MN 55605-3000

Closest City or Town: Grand Portage, Minnesota

How to Get There: Take State Highway 61 north to the park entrance, just before the Canadian border.

GPS Coordinates: 48.0005579° N, 89.5931273° W

Best Time to Visit: Spring through fall

Pass/Permit/Fees: Free

Did You Know? Grand Portage State Park is the only Minnesota state park jointly managed with a Native American tribe, the Grand Portage Band of Chippewa.

Website:
http://www.dnr.state.mn.us/state_parks/grand_portage/index.html

GRAND MARAIS

Niagara Cave

Descend into a subterranean wonder at Niagara Cave in Harmony, Minnesota. This awe-inspiring cave features an underground waterfall, fossils over 450 million years old, and stunning formations like stalactites and flowstones. Guided tours offer fascinating insights into geology and the cave's natural history. Located in southeastern Minnesota, it's a must-visit for spelunkers and nature enthusiasts.

Location: 29842 County 30, Harmony, MN 55939-4520

Closest City or Town: Harmony, Minnesota

How to Get There: From Harmony, take State Highway 52 south to County Road 30, then follow signs to the cave.

GPS Coordinates: 43.5143070° N, 92.0547750° W

Best Time to Visit: Spring through fall

Pass/Permit/Fees: $11-$15, varying by age group

Did You Know? Niagara Cave remains a constant 48 degrees Fahrenheit year-round, making it a cool escape even in summer.

Website: http://www.niagaracave.com/

LUTSEN

Cascade River State Park

Find your sense of adventure amidst the captivating landscapes of Cascade River State Park in Lutsen, Minnesota. This scenic park is nestled along Lake Superior's North Shore and is renowned for its stunning waterfalls, rugged river gorges, and lush forests. Visitors can hike the network of trails that lead to breathtaking viewpoints, picnic by the cascading waters, and explore the diverse flora and fauna that make this park a natural gem. The park's unique feature is the endless series of waterfalls that create a mesmerizing symphony of nature, perfect for photography enthusiasts and nature lovers.

Location: 3481 W Highway 61, Lutsen, MN 55612-9535

Closest City or Town: Lutsen, Minnesota

How to Get There: Take Hwy 61 North from Duluth for 108 miles. The park entrance is located right off the highway and is well-marked.

GPS Coordinates: 47.7158205° N, 90.5168684° W

Best Time to Visit: Spring through fall for hiking and waterfall views; winter for snowshoeing.

Pass/Permit/Fees: State park vehicle permit required.

Did You Know? The park's river and waterfall system plunge a combined 900 feet from the highest falls to the river mouth at Lake Superior.

Website:
http://www.dnr.state.mn.us/state_parks/cascade_river/index.html

Lutsen Mountains Ski & Summer Resort

Experience the thrill and beauty of the seasons at Lutsen Mountains Ski & Summer Resort, nestled in Lutsen, Minnesota. Renowned as one of the premier outdoor adventure destinations in the Midwest, this resort offers a wealth of activities year-round. In winter, ski or snowboard down over 90 runs across four interconnected peaks, and in summer, enjoy mountain biking, hiking, or a scenic gondola ride.

Located along the majestic Sawtooth Mountains and overlooking Lake Superior, the resort's unique feature is its stunning panoramic view, offering a breathtaking backdrop for all your adventures.

Location: 467 Ski Hill Road, Lutsen, MN 55612

Closest City or Town: Lutsen, Minnesota

How to Get There: From Duluth, take Hwy 61 for about 95 miles north to Lutsen, then turn onto Ski Hill Road.

GPS Coordinates: 47.6637130° N, 90.7135557° W

Best Time to Visit: Winter for skiing and snowboarding; summer for hiking and mountain biking.

Pass/Permit/Fees: Varies by activity; lift tickets and passes required for winter sports.

Did You Know? Lutsen Mountains features the Midwest's only gondola, which offers spectacular views of the surrounding area.

Website: http://www.lutsen.com/

MANKATO

Minneopa State Park

Step into a world of natural wonder at Minneopa State Park in Mankato, Minnesota. This charming park features the stunning Minneopa Falls, a two-tiered waterfall that offers a breathtaking spectacle. Visitors can hike nature trails, encounter the park's bison herd in the Minneopa Prairie, and explore the historical Seppmann Mill. Located near the Minnesota River, the park's unique feature is its combination of scenic beauty and rich history, making it a perfect destination for both relaxation and exploration.

Location: 54497 Gadwall Rd, Mankato, MN 56001-5929

Closest City or Town: Mankato, Minnesota

How to Get There: From Hwy 169, take the turnoff for Hwy 68 West and then follow signs to the park entrance.

GPS Coordinates: 44.1478375° N, 94.0952120° W

Best Time to Visit: Spring through fall for hiking and waterfall viewing; winter for snow activities.

Pass/Permit/Fees: State park vehicle permit required.

Did You Know? The name Minneopa means water falling twice in Dakota, referring to the park's iconic two-tiered waterfall.

Website:
http://www.dnr.state.mn.us/state_parks/minneopa/index.html

Sibley Park

Rediscover a blend of history and beauty at Sibley Park in Mankato, Minnesota. This enchanting park, nestled along the Minnesota River, is a haven of tranquility with beautifully manicured gardens, family-friendly picnic areas, and a petting zoo. Visitors can enjoy scenic walks, watch local wildlife, and participate in seasonal events. The park is named after Henry Hastings Sibley, Minnesota's first governor. Its unique feature is the charming petting zoo, which offers fun interactions with farm animals, making it a perfect spot for families and nature enthusiasts.

Location: 900 Mound Ave, Mankato, MN 56001

Closest City or Town: Mankato, Minnesota

How to Get There: From Hwy 169, take the Riverfront Dr exit, follow south to Sibley Parkway, and then to Mound Ave.

GPS Coordinates: 44.1615061° N, 94.0329562° W

Best Time to Visit: Spring through fall for garden blooms and family activities.

Pass/Permit/Fees: Free

Did You Know? Sibley Park's annual Kiwanis Holiday Lights event transforms the park with over 1.5 million lights.

Website:

http://www.mankato-mn.gov/Wishbook/SibleyParkZoo.aspx

MINNEAPOLIS

American Swedish Institute

Discover a blend of Nordic culture and architectural beauty at the American Swedish Institute in Minneapolis, Minnesota. Housed in the stunning Turnblad Mansion, this cultural center offers vibrant exhibits, engaging programs, and traditional Swedish events. Wander through the elegantly designed rooms and admire artifacts that tell the story of Swedish-American heritage. From intricate woodwork to colorful folk art, there's a rich tapestry of history and culture waiting to be explored.

Location: 2600 Park Ave, Minneapolis, MN 55407-1090

Closest City or Town: Minneapolis, Minnesota

How to Get There: Easily accessible from Interstate 35W, take the exit for E 26th St and follow it to Park Ave.

GPS Coordinates: 44.9545975° N, 93.2658596° W

Best Time to Visit: Year-round, with special events during Swedish holidays.

Pass/Permit/Fees: Admission fees vary; see the website for details.

Did You Know? The Turnblad Mansion features 33 rooms with eleven porcelain tile stoves, all imported from Sweden.

Website: https://asimn.org/

Basilica of St. Mary

Step into the spiritual grandeur of the Basilica of St. Mary, located in Minneapolis, Minnesota. This magnificent basilica, with its stunning Beaux-Arts architecture, intricate stained glass windows, and awe-inspiring altar, offers a serene space for reflection and prayer. As the first basilica established in the United States, it stands as a testament to religious artistry and community dedication.

Location: 88 N 17th St, Minneapolis, MN 55403-1295

Closest City or Town: Minneapolis, Minnesota

How to Get There: From I-394, take the exit for Dunwoody Blvd and follow signs to Basilica of St. Mary.

GPS Coordinates: 44.9730524° N, 93.2862357° W

Best Time to Visit: Year-round

Pass/Permit/Fees: Free

Did You Know? The Basilica of St. Mary hosts the annual Basilica Block Party, a music festival that has become a summer tradition in Minneapolis.

Website: http://www.mary.org/

Bde Maka Ska

Immerse yourself in the natural beauty and recreational opportunities at Bde Maka Ska, the largest lake in Minneapolis, Minnesota. Kayak on its calm waters, bike along the scenic trails, or relax on the sandy beaches. This urban oasis offers a perfect blend of outdoor activities and serene spaces, ideal for both adventure seekers and those looking to unwind.

Location: West Lake St and Calhoun Parkway, Minneapolis, MN 55408

Closest City or Town: Minneapolis, Minnesota

How to Get There: Accessible via Excelsior Blvd, then follow signs to Bde Maka Ska.

GPS Coordinates: 44.9481637° N, 93.3065193° W

Best Time to Visit: Summer for water activities; autumn for stunning foliage.

Pass/Permit/Fees: Free

Did You Know? Bde Maka Ska means Lake White Earth in the Dakota language and reflects the lake's cultural significance.

Website:
http://www.minneapolisparks.org/parks__destinations/parks__lakes/bde_maka_ska_park/

Foshay Tower

Discover breathtaking city views and historical elegance at the Foshay Tower in Minneapolis, Minnesota. Once the tallest building in the city, this Art Deco gem features an observation deck offering stunning panoramic vistas. Explore the museum inside, which chronicles the tower's captivating history and its visionary founder, Wilbur Foshay.

Location: 821 Marquette Ave, Minneapolis, MN 55402-2929

Closest City or Town: Minneapolis, Minnesota

How to Get There: Located downtown, accessible via 8th St or Marquette Ave.

GPS Coordinates: 44.9747324° N, 93.2720141° W

Best Time to Visit: Year-round, with clear days offering the best views.

Pass/Permit/Fees: Admission fees apply; check the website for details.

Did You Know? The Foshay Tower was inspired by the Washington Monument and remains one of the few examples of Art Deco architecture in the region.

Website:

https://www.exploreminnesota.com/profile/foshay-museum-observation-deck/3510

Grand Rounds Scenic Byway

Experience the natural splendor of Minneapolis via the Grand Rounds Scenic Byway, a network of picturesque parkways and trails. This unique urban byway loops around lakes, gardens, and riverbanks, offering ample opportunities for biking, running, and picturesque drives. Uncover the city's green heart through its interconnected parks and lush landscapes.

Location: 400 S 4th St, Minneapolis, MN 55415-1411

Closest City or Town: Minneapolis, Minnesota

How to Get There: Best accessed via any major roadways intersecting Minneapolis, including I-35W and Hennepin Ave.

GPS Coordinates: 44.9776194° N, 93.2636967° W

Best Time to Visit: Spring through fall for the full outdoor experience.

Pass/Permit/Fees: Free

Did You Know? The Grand Rounds Scenic Byway spans over 50 miles, making it one of the longest continuous urban parkway systems in the country.

Website: http://www.minneapolisparks.org/parks-destinations/trails-parkways/grand_rounds_scenic_byway_system/

Huntington Bank Stadium

Feel the energy and excitement at Huntington Bank Stadium, the vibrant home of the University of Minnesota Golden Gophers in Minneapolis. This state-of-the-art stadium, filled with enthusiastic fans, offers a thrilling game day experience. Catch a football game and revel in the electrifying atmosphere while enjoying views of the Minneapolis skyline.

Location: 420 23rd Ave SE, Minneapolis, MN 55455-3026

Closest City or Town: Minneapolis, Minnesota

How to Get There: Accessible from I-35W, take the University Ave SE exit and follow signs to the stadium.

GPS Coordinates: 44.9765250° N, 93.2245462° W

Best Time to Visit: Fall during football season for a memorable game day experience.

Pass/Permit/Fees: Ticket prices vary by event; check the website for details.

Did You Know? The stadium is designed to hold over 50,000 fans and features a unique brick and mortar exterior paying homage to the historic campus architecture.

Website: https://gophersports.com/sports/2022/10/18/huntington-bank-stadium

Lake Harriet

Discover tranquility at Lake Harriet, a serene gem nestled in the heart of Minneapolis. This picturesque lake offers a blend of outdoor activities, including fishing, canoeing, and walking along its scenic trails. During summer months, enjoy live concerts and movies at the charming bandshell, surrounded by lush greenery.

Location: West 42nd St and West Lake Harriet Parkway, Minneapolis, MN 55409

Closest City or Town: Minneapolis, Minnesota

How to Get There: From I-35W, take the 46th St exit, head west on 46th St, then turn right onto Lake Harriet Parkway.

GPS Coordinates: 44.9220643° N, 93.3046656° W

Best Time to Visit: Summer for concerts and outdoor activities; fall for beautiful foliage.

Pass/Permit/Fees: Free

Did You Know? Lake Harriet is one of three interconnected lakes along the Grand Rounds Scenic Byway, offering an extensive network of trails.

Website:

https://www.minneapolisparks.org/parks-destinations/parks-lakes/lake_harriet_park

Lake of the Isles

Experience the natural beauty of Lake of the Isles, a beloved spot in Minneapolis known for its charming islands and picturesque views. Visitors can kayak, paddleboard, or bike along the winding paths that border the lake. In winter, enjoy ice skating and hockey; it's a year-round haven for outdoor enthusiasts.

Location: 2500 W Lake of the Isles Pkwy Franklin Ave and Logan Ave South, Minneapolis, MN 55405-2332

Closest City or Town: Minneapolis, Minnesota

How to Get There: From I-394, take the Penn Ave exit south, then turn east onto Lake of the Isles Parkway.

GPS Coordinates: 44.9630220° N, 93.3042075° W

Best Time to Visit: Spring through fall for water activities; winter for ice sports.

Pass/Permit/Fees: Free

Did You Know? Lake of the Isles is connected to the Minneapolis Chain of Lakes, which includes Bde Maka Ska and Lake Harriet, forming a popular loop for recreational activities.

Website: http://www.minneapolisparks.org/parks_and_destinations/parks_an d_lakes/lake_of_the_isles_park/#group_1_13979

Loring Park

Located in the heart of Minneapolis, Loring Park is a haven of lush greenery and cultural vibrancy. This beloved urban park features beautiful walking paths, a serene pond, and the lively Loring Park Art Festival. It's perfect for a peaceful stroll, a picnic, or an exploration of local art and community events.

Location: 1382 Willow St July 30-31,2016, Minneapolis, MN 55403-2256

Closest City or Town: Minneapolis, Minnesota

How to Get There: From I-94, take the Hennepin/Lyndale exit, and head south on Lyndale. Follow signs to the park.

GPS Coordinates: 44.9688740° N, 93.2827787° W

Best Time to Visit: Summer for festivals and events; fall for the beautiful colors.

Pass/Permit/Fees: Free

Did You Know? Loring Park was established in 1883 and is home to several historic statues, including the statue of Ole Bull, a renowned Norwegian violinist.

Website: http://www.loringparkartfestival.com/

Mill City Museum

Embark on a historical journey at the Mill City Museum in the bustling Mill District of Minneapolis. Built on the ruins of what was once the world's largest flour mill, this museum offers interactive exhibits showcasing the milling industry's heritage and its impact on the city. Enjoy panoramic views of the Mississippi River from the rooftop observation deck.

Location: 704 S 2nd St, Minneapolis, MN 55401-2163

Closest City or Town: Minneapolis, Minnesota

How to Get There: From I-35W, take the Washington Ave exit, head east, and turn right onto S 2nd St.

GPS Coordinates: 44.9787828° N, 93.2572710° W

Best Time to Visit: Year-round, with special events during summer.

Pass/Permit/Fees: $6-$12, varying by age.

Did You Know? The museum's Flour Tower elevator ride brings visitors through the mill's history with multi-sensory theatrics.

Website: http://www.mnhs.org/millcity

Minneapolis Institute of Art

Embark on a journey through time and creativity at the Minneapolis Institute of Art, where over 89,000 artworks spanning 5,000 years are waiting to dazzle visitors. Marvel at masterpieces from diverse cultures, delve into stunning exhibits of sculptures, paintings, textiles, and photography. This impressive cultural treasure trove is located in the heart of Minneapolis, making it a vibrant hub for art lovers and curious minds alike.

Location: 2400 Third Avenue South, Minneapolis, MN 55404-3506

Closest City or Town: Minneapolis, Minnesota

How to Get There: Easily accessible from Interstate 35W, take the exit for E 24th St and follow it to Third Avenue South.

GPS Coordinates: 44.9585890° N, 93.2742238° W

Best Time to Visit: Year-round

Pass/Permit/Fees: Free, with some special exhibits requiring a fee

Did You Know? The Institute's collection includes one of the largest and most comprehensive collections of Asian art in the United States.

Website: http://www.artsmia.org/

Minneapolis Sculpture Garden

Discover the intersection of nature and art at the Minneapolis Sculpture Garden, an enchanting outdoor gallery that brings creativity into the open air. Spanning 11 acres, the garden features iconic sculptures like the Spoonbridge and Cherry. Stroll among fascinating works of art and lush greenery in this urban oasis, located next to the Walker Art Center.

Location: 725 Vineland Place, Minneapolis, MN 55403

Closest City or Town: Minneapolis, Minnesota

How to Get There: Accessible from I-94, take the Lyndale Ave exit and follow signs to Vineland Place.

GPS Coordinates: 44.9695479° N, 93.2897803° W

Best Time to Visit: Spring through fall for optimal weather

Pass/Permit/Fees: Free

Did You Know? The garden is home to over 40 artworks from prominent artists, including the renowned Arikidea by Mark di Suvero.

Website: http://www.walkerart.org/garden/

Minneapolis Skyway System

Navigate the city in a unique way with the Minneapolis Skyway System, a network of enclosed pedestrian footbridges connecting buildings throughout downtown Minneapolis. Spanning nine miles, this climate-controlled marvel is perfect for exploring shops, restaurants, and attractions without braving the weather.

Location: 101 S 7th St, Minneapolis, MN 55402

Closest City or Town: Minneapolis, Minnesota

How to Get There: Located in downtown Minneapolis, accessible via major roadways like Hennepin Ave and Nicollet Mall.

GPS Coordinates: 44.9760679° N, 93.2702820° W

Best Time to Visit: Year-round, especially during winter months

Pass/Permit/Fees: Free

Did You Know? The Skyway System is one of the largest interconnected systems of its kind in the world, covering 80 city blocks.

Website:
https://www.minneapolis.org/map-transportation/minneapolis-skyway-guide/

Minnehaha Falls

Experience the breathtaking beauty of Minnehaha Falls, a majestic 53-foot waterfall cascading in the scenic Minnehaha Park. This natural wonder invites visitors to explore surrounding walking trails, enjoy picnics, and revel in the serene ambiance of one of Minneapolis's most cherished landmarks.

Location: 4801 S Minnehaha Drive, Minneapolis, MN 55417

Closest City or Town: Minneapolis, Minnesota

How to Get There: From Highway 55, head east on Minnehaha Avenue and follow signs to the park entrance.

GPS Coordinates: 44.9153506° N, 93.2110082° W

Best Time to Visit: Spring through fall for optimal waterfall viewing; winter to see the frozen falls

Pass/Permit/Fees: Free

Did You Know? Minnehaha Falls was made famous by Henry Wadsworth Longfellow's epic poem The Song of Hiawatha.

Website: https://www.minneapolisparks.org/parks-destinations/parks-lakes/minnehaha_regional_park

Minnehaha Park

Immerse yourself in the natural splendor of Minnehaha Park, a 193-acre sanctuary in Minneapolis that boasts abundant greenery, historic sites, and the spectacular Minnehaha Falls. Enjoy activities like hiking, cycling, picnicking, and guided historical tours, making it a favorite destination for nature enthusiasts and families alike.

Location: 4801 Minnehaha Ave, Minneapolis, MN 55417-2373

Closest City or Town: Minneapolis, Minnesota

How to Get There: Easily reachable from Highway 55, take the Minnehaha Ave exit, then follow signs to the park.

GPS Coordinates: 44.9168576° N, 93.2130061° W

Best Time to Visit: Spring through fall for best outdoor experiences; winter to enjoy the frozen waterfall

Pass/Permit/Fees: Free

Did You Know? The park is home to several historical sites, including the John H. Stevens House, one of the first houses built in Minneapolis.

Website:
http://www.minneapolisparks.org/parks__destinations/parks__lakes/minnehaha_regional_park/

Nicollet Mall

Step into one of Minneapolis's most vibrant urban landscapes at Nicollet Mall, a bustling thoroughfare in the heart of downtown. This pedestrian-friendly street is home to an array of shops, cafes, restaurants, and public art installations. Located between Washington Avenue and Grant Street, Nicollet Mall has been a central hub of activity since its creation in the 1960s. Visitors can enjoy al fresco dining, shop for unique finds, or admire the many public art pieces that dot the landscape. During the winter, the twinkling lights provide a magical atmosphere, and in summer, it becomes a lively scene of outdoor activities.

Location: 800 Nicollet Mall, Minneapolis, MN 55402

Closest City or Town: Minneapolis, Minnesota

How to Get There: Accessible via Metro Transit or by car, with ample parking available in nearby garages.

GPS Coordinates: 44.9755906° N, 93.2738748° W

Best Time to Visit: Year-round, with special events held throughout the year.

Pass/Permit/Fees: Free

Did You Know? Nicollet Mall underwent a $50 million renovation that was completed in 2017, modernizing it while maintaining its historic charm.

Website: http://www.minneapolis.org/visitor/shopping/nicollet-mall

St. Anthony Falls

Experience the natural beauty and historical significance at St. Anthony Falls, located on the Mississippi River in Minneapolis. Known as the only natural major waterfall on the Mississippi, its rushing waters were once central to the city's flour milling industry. The falls can be easily accessed from Mill Ruins Park, providing picturesque views and a scenic backdrop for walks. Visitors can explore the surrounding parks, take a riverboat tour, or visit the nearby Stone Arch Bridge for panoramic photos. Rich in both natural beauty and history, it's a must-see destination for any traveler.

Location: West River Road and Portland Ave, Minneapolis, MN 55414

Closest City or Town: Minneapolis, Minnesota

How to Get There: Reach the falls by heading east from downtown on Portland Ave, which merges onto West River Road.

GPS Coordinates: 44.9784592° N, 93.2471880° W

Best Time to Visit: Spring through fall for the best river views and weather.

Pass/Permit/Fees: Free

Did You Know? St. Anthony Falls is named after Saint Anthony of Padua and was a crucial factor in Minneapolis becoming a milling powerhouse in the 19th century.

Website: http://www.nps.gov/miss/planyourvisit/uppestan.htm

The Museum of Russian Art

Explore the rich cultural tapestry of Russia at The Museum of Russian Art in Minneapolis. This unique museum, housed in a beautifully converted church, features rotating exhibits of Russian art and artifacts spanning centuries. From classical paintings to Soviet-era propaganda posters, the collection provides a deep dive into

Russian history and culture. Located in the Kingfield neighborhood, it's an intimate museum that offers an enlightening and often surprising look at Russian artistry.

Location: 5500 Stevens Ave, Minneapolis, MN 55419-1933

Closest City or Town: Minneapolis, Minnesota

How to Get There: Accessible from I-35W, take the 46th St exit and head south on Stevens Ave.

GPS Coordinates: 44.9033691° N, 93.2759371° W

Best Time to Visit: Year-round, with new exhibits and seasonal events.

Pass/Permit/Fees: $5-$15, depending on age and membership status.

Did You Know? The Museum of Russian Art is the only museum in North America dedicated exclusively to Russian art.

Website: http://tmora.org/

U.S. Bank Stadium

Feel the excitement of the NFL at U.S. Bank Stadium, home to the Minnesota Vikings. This state-of-the-art facility in downtown Minneapolis offers not just football games but concerts, sporting events, and more. Its striking architecture, complete with a transparent roof and pivoting doors, makes it a marvel to behold. Beyond game day, take a tour to explore the stadium's unique features and behind-the-scenes areas. With its location near the downtown core, it's easily accessible and close to many other attractions.

Location: 401 Chicago Ave, Minneapolis, MN 55415-1515

Closest City or Town: Minneapolis, Minnesota

How to Get There: Take I-94 and exit at 11th St, then head east on Chicago Ave.

GPS Coordinates: 44.9736461° N, 93.2574945° W

Best Time to Visit: Fall for football games, but open year-round for tours and events.

Pass/Permit/Fees: Ticket prices vary. Stadium tours typically cost $10-$20.

Did You Know? U.S. Bank Stadium hosted Super Bowl LII in 2018, which saw the Philadelphia Eagles defeat the New England Patriots.

Website: http://www.usbankstadium.com/

University of Minnesota

Delve into the academic and cultural heart of Minnesota at the University of Minnesota in Minneapolis. With its sprawling campus along the Mississippi River, this university offers a blend of top-tier educational facilities, lush green spaces, and vibrant urban life. Visitors can enjoy walking tours, engage in campus events, and explore museums like the Weisman Art Museum. The university's iconic buildings and scenic riverfront provide a picturesque setting that encapsulates the spirit of academia and community.

Location: 100 Church Street SE Between Mississippi and University Aves, Minneapolis, MN 55455

Closest City or Town: Minneapolis, Minnesota

How to Get There: From I-35W, take the University Ave SE exit, head east, and follow signs to the university's main campus.

GPS Coordinates: 44.9789666° N, 93.2351854° W

Best Time to Visit: Spring and fall for campus events and beautiful scenery

Pass/Permit/Fees: Free

Did You Know? The university is home to the Bell Museum, Minnesota's official natural history museum.

Website: https://twin-cities.umn.edu/

Uptown

Immerse yourself in the eclectic atmosphere of Uptown, a lively neighborhood in Minneapolis. Known for its mix of trendy boutiques, vibrant nightlife, and artistic flair, Uptown offers an array of activities from shopping at local stores to dining at diverse restaurants. Take a stroll around Lake Calhoun or catch a film at the historic Uptown

Theater. This urban hub serves as a melting pot of culture and creativity, making it a vibrant destination for all.

Location: 3001 Hennepin Avenue South, Minneapolis, MN 55408

Closest City or Town: Minneapolis, Minnesota

How to Get There: From I-94, take the Lyndale Ave exit and head south to Hennepin Ave, then follow signs to Uptown.

GPS Coordinates: 44.9475700° N, 93.2976669° W

Best Time to Visit: Summer for outdoor festivals and bustling streets

Pass/Permit/Fees: Free

Did You Know? Uptown hosts the annual Uptown Art Fair, which attracts hundreds of thousands of visitors each year.

Website: http://www.uptownminneapolis.com/

Walker Art Center

Explore cutting-edge contemporary art at the Walker Art Center in Minneapolis. Renowned for its dynamic exhibitions, this museum showcases works from leading artists across various disciplines. Visitors can wander through the outdoor Minneapolis Sculpture Garden, home to the iconic Spoonbridge and Cherry. With its innovative programs and striking architecture, the Walker Art Center stands as a beacon of modern art and cultural exploration.

Location: 725 Vineland Pl, Minneapolis, MN 55403-1195

Closest City or Town: Minneapolis, Minnesota

How to Get There: From I-94, take the Hennepin/Lyndale Ave exit, follow Vineland Pl to the museum's entrance.

GPS Coordinates: 44.9681442° N, 93.2886494° W

Best Time to Visit: Year-round, with outdoor garden best enjoyed in spring and summer

Pass/Permit/Fees: Admission fees apply; check the website for details.

Did You Know? The Minneapolis Sculpture Garden, adjacent to the Walker, features over 40 outdoor artworks.

Website: https://walkerart.org/

Weisman Art Museum

Step into a world of artistic innovation at the Weisman Art Museum, located on the University of Minnesota campus in Minneapolis. Designed by famed architect Frank Gehry, the museum exhibits a diverse collection of modern art, ceramics, and American folk art. The striking stainless steel structure itself is a work of art, drawing visitors for its architectural marvel and eclectic exhibitions.

Location: 333 E River Pkwy, Minneapolis, MN 55455-0367

Closest City or Town: Minneapolis, Minnesota

How to Get There: From I-35W, take the University Ave SE exit, head east, and follow the signs to the museum along River Parkway.

GPS Coordinates: 44.9731104° N, 93.2369351° W

Best Time to Visit: Year-round

Pass/Permit/Fees: Free

Did You Know? The museum's design includes a blend of curving and angular shapes, making it a landmark on the Mississippi River.

Website:
https://wam.umn.edu/?fbclid=IwAR0_gVqg5EBIx0HNZZV5fgQOELJ_t
NInNsyGKUneX29I0jAefdkI0LTCUk0_aem_AYofuXN8agYWAP8oniovw
FJDSPN8cCGIZN_VISXId1-
AcShwyxZ3OP0k31V9mbW29nVsIQ5ZJ_HFTP8sgcEjoTVO

MOORHEAD

Historical and Cultural Society of Clay County

Dive into the rich history and culture of Clay County at the Historical and Cultural Society, housed in the Hjemkomst Center in Moorhead. This museum offers engaging exhibits that chronicle the local heritage, including a magnificent Viking ship replica. Wander through informative displays that explore the area's diverse cultural roots and historical milestones. A visit here provides a unique glimpse into the past, making it a must-see for history buffs.

Location: 202 1st Ave N The Hjemkomst Center, Moorhead, MN 56560-1985

Closest City or Town: Moorhead, Minnesota

How to Get There: Head north on 1st Ave N from downtown Moorhead; the center is just a few minutes away.

GPS Coordinates: 46.8779068° N, 96.7784035° W

Best Time to Visit: Year-round, with special events in the summer

Pass/Permit/Fees: Entry fees vary; see the website for details.

Did You Know? The Hjemkomst Viking Ship was built by Robert Asp and sailed from Minnesota to Norway.

Website: https://www.hcscconline.org/

NEW ULM

Hermann the German

Standing proudly in New Ulm, Hermann the German symbolizes freedom and German-American heritage. This imposing statue offers breathtaking views of the surrounding countryside and commemorates the Germanic warrior, Arminius. Climb to the top for a panoramic vista, or explore the surrounding Hermann Heights Park, making it a memorable stop for history enthusiasts.

Location: 10 Monument St, New Ulm, MN 56073

Closest City or Town: New Ulm, Minnesota

How to Get There: From downtown New Ulm, head west on Center Street and follow signs to the monument.

GPS Coordinates: 44.3071056° N, 94.4728611° W

Best Time to Visit: Spring through fall for the best views

Pass/Permit/Fees: Free

Did You Know? The monument is a replica of the famed Hermannsdenkmal in Detmold, Germany.

Website: http://hermannmonument.com/

Schell's Brewery

Discover the charm and history of Schell's Brewery, nestled in New Ulm. Established in 1860, it's one of the oldest family-owned breweries in the United States. Embark on a brewery tour to see the historic brewing process, enjoy tastings of their finest beers, and explore the beautiful gardens. It's an unforgettable experience for craft beer aficionados and history lovers alike.

Location: 1860 Schells Rd, New Ulm, MN 56073-3834

Closest City or Town: New Ulm, Minnesota

MINNESOTA BUCKET LIST

How to Get There: Travel south from downtown New Ulm on Broadway St, then turn right onto 16th St S and follow signs to the brewery.

GPS Coordinates: 44.2893797° N, 94.4499494° W

Best Time to Visit: Year-round, with the summer offering beautiful garden views

Pass/Permit/Fees: Admission fees apply for tours and tastings; check the website for details.

Did You Know? The brewery survived Prohibition by producing non-alcoholic beverages and near beer.

Website:
https://en.wikipedia.org/wiki/August_Schell_Brewing_Company

ORR

Vince Shute Wildlife Sanctuary

Immerse yourself in the wonders of wildlife at the Vince Shute Wildlife Sanctuary in Orr. Known as the Sanctuary of the American Bear, this site offers unique opportunities to observe and photograph black bears in their natural habitat. Guided tours and educational programs provide insights into bear behavior and conservation, making it a captivating experience for nature lovers and photographers.

Location: 12541 Nett Lake Rd, Orr, MN 55771

Closest City or Town: Orr, Minnesota

How to Get There: From downtown Orr, head northwest on US-53, then turn left onto Nett Lake Rd and follow signs to the sanctuary.

GPS Coordinates: 48.0887330° N, 93.0177040° W

Best Time to Visit: Summer for the best chance to see bears

Pass/Permit/Fees: Admission fees apply; see the website for current rates.

Did You Know? The sanctuary was founded by Vince Shute, who observed black bears for over 30 years.

Website: http://www.americanbear.org/

PARK RAPIDS

Itasca State Park

Find your sense of adventure at Itasca State Park, where you can walk across the source of the Mississippi River. Located in Park Rapids, this stunning park is known for its ancient pine trees, scenic trails, and the historic Douglas Lodge. Visitors can enjoy hiking, boating, and bird-watching in this serene natural setting. Don't miss the chance to dip your toes in the headwaters of America's iconic river.

Location: 36750 Main Park Dr Intersection of Hwy 71 and Hwy 200 West, Park Rapids, MN 56470-9722

Closest City or Town: Park Rapids, Minnesota

How to Get There: Take Highway 71 north from Park Rapids, following signs to the park entrance.

GPS Coordinates: 47.2176584° N, 95.1802980° W

Best Time to Visit: Summer for outdoor activities and fall for foliage

Pass/Permit/Fees: State park vehicle permit required

Did You Know? Itasca State Park is Minnesota's oldest state park, established in 1891.

Website: http://www.dnr.state.mn.us/state_parks/itasca/index.html

PIPESTONE

Pipestone National Monument

Discover the rich cultural heritage and natural beauty at Pipestone National Monument in Pipestone, Minnesota. This sacred site has been used by Native Americans for centuries to quarry the distinctive red pipestone for making ceremonial pipes. Visitors can explore the picturesque landscapes, walk along self-guided trails, and witness traditional pipestone carving demonstrations. The site features stunning rock formations, waterfalls, and prairie landscapes. The unique combination of natural beauty and profound cultural significance makes this a must-see destination for history enthusiasts and nature lovers.

Location: 36 Reservation Ave, Pipestone, MN 56164

Closest City or Town: Pipestone, Minnesota

How to Get There: From US-75, take the exit for MN-30 E and follow signs to Pipestone National Monument.

GPS Coordinates: 44.0133193° N, 96.3252011° W

Best Time to Visit: Spring through fall for the best weather and activities.

Pass/Permit/Fees: Entrance fees apply; see website for details.

Did You Know? The monument is home to several endangered plant and animal species, making it an important ecological site.

Website: http://www.nps.gov/pipe/index.htm

PRESTON

Forestville/Mystery Cave State Park

Unearth natural wonders and historical intrigue at Forestville/Mystery Cave State Park in Preston, Minnesota. This fascinating state park offers diverse experiences, from exploring Minnesota's longest cave system adorned with stunning formations to visiting the Historic Forestville living-history site which reconstructs 19th-century village life. Perfect for outdoor enthusiasts, you can enjoy hiking, fishing, and picnicking amidst picturesque landscapes. The park's unique blend of geological marvels and historical reenactments provides an enriching adventure for all ages.

Location: 21071 County 118, Preston, MN 55965-4502

Closest City or Town: Preston, Minnesota

How to Get There: Take Highway 16 into Preston, then follow County Road 5 S to County Road 118 E.

GPS Coordinates: 43.6377910° N, 92.2192360° W

Best Time to Visit: Spring through fall for outdoor activities and tours.

Pass/Permit/Fees: State park vehicle permit required.

Did You Know? The Mystery Cave system stretches for over 13 miles underground.

Website:
http://www.dnr.state.mn.us/state_parks/park.html?id=spk00148#homepage

RED WING

Barn Bluff

Soak in stunning vistas and rich history at Barn Bluff in Red Wing, Minnesota. This prominent river bluff offers challenging hiking trails that reward climbers with panoramic views of the Mississippi River and surrounding town. Known for its historical significance and natural beauty, Barn Bluff has long been a landmark for Native Americans and early explorers. Whether you're a hiking enthusiast or history buff, the blend of scenic trails and historical markers make this a captivating destination.

Location: Barn Bluff Trail Start, 602 Centennial St, Red Wing, MN 55066

Closest City or Town: Red Wing, Minnesota

How to Get There: Take US-61 into Red Wing, turn onto Main St and follow signs to the Barn Bluff trailhead.

GPS Coordinates: 44.5682667° N, 92.5181752° W

Best Time to Visit: Spring through fall for hiking; winter for cross-country skiing.

Pass/Permit/Fees: Free

Did You Know? Legend says that Barn Bluff was once an island in the Mississippi River.

Website: http://www.red-wing.org/barnbluff.html

Pottery Museum of Red Wing

Step into a world of artistic craftsmanship at the Pottery Museum of Red Wing in Red Wing, Minnesota. This impressive museum showcases over 6,000 unique pieces of Red Wing pottery and stoneware, reflecting the region's rich ceramic heritage. Visitors can marvel at beautifully crafted pieces, from utilitarian stoneware to elegant art pottery. Located in the heart of pottery country, this museum offers a deep dive into the history and artistry that made Red Wing pottery famous.

Location: 240 Harrison St, Red Wing, MN 55066-2085

Closest City or Town: Red Wing, Minnesota

How to Get There: Accessible via US-61; turn onto Main St and follow directions to Harrison St.

GPS Coordinates: 44.5633579° N, 92.5590500° W

Best Time to Visit: Year-round

Pass/Permit/Fees: Free

Did You Know? The museum features the largest known collection of Red Wing pottery in the world.

Website: https://potterymuseumredwing.org/

Red Wing Shoe Store & Museum

Explore the legacy of craftsmanship at the Red Wing Shoe Store & Museum in Red Wing, Minnesota. Home to the iconic Red Wing boots, this museum offers an intriguing look into the history of the renowned brand. Visitors can tour exhibits showcasing boot-making processes, original designs, and the world's largest boot, a must-see attraction at over 20 feet tall. Situated in a beautifully restored historic building, the museum provides a nostalgic journey through time for footwear fans and history buffs alike.

Location: 315 Main St, Red Wing, MN 55066-2322

Closest City or Town: Red Wing, Minnesota

How to Get There: Located directly on Main St, easily accessible from US-61.

GPS Coordinates: 44.5660962° N, 92.5343789° W

Best Time to Visit: Year-round

Pass/Permit/Fees: Free

Did You Know? The Red Wing Shoe Store's giant boot is a size 638 ½ D and weighs over 2,300 pounds.

Website: https://stores.redwingshoes.com/red-wing-mn

ROCHESTER

Mayowood Historic Home

Step back in time and explore the elegant Mayowood Historic Home, a testament to the Mayo family's legacy in Rochester, Minnesota. This grand estate, with its stunning gardens and rich history, offers insights into the lives of Dr. Charles Mayo and his family. Visitors can tour the meticulously preserved mansion, filled with original furnishings and artifacts, and stroll through the picturesque grounds. Highlights include the beautiful conservatory and scenic river views, making it a perfect blend of history and nature.

Location: 1195 West Circle Drive SW, Rochester, MN 55902-4260

Closest City or Town: Rochester, Minnesota

How to Get There: From US Highway 52, take exit 56C and follow 2nd St SW west, then turn left onto Mayowood Road SW and follow signs to the estate.

GPS Coordinates: 44.0063125° N, 92.5098776° W

Best Time to Visit: Spring and fall for the best weather and garden views

Pass/Permit/Fees: Admission fees apply; check the website for details.

Did You Know? Mayowood was built in 1911 and showcases over ten rooms decorated in various historical styles.

Website: https://www.olmstedhistory.com/mayowood/

Plummer House

Explore the grandeur of the Plummer House, a historical gem nestled in the heart of Rochester, Minnesota. Built in 1924 by Dr. Henry Plummer, this mansion boasts Tudor-style architecture, beautiful gardens, and intricate interior details. Visitors can tour the home, wander through five acres of landscaped grounds, and admire the historic water tower. Unique features include hidden passageways and stunning oak woodwork, making it a fascinating destination for history enthusiasts and architecture buffs alike.

Location: 1091 Plummer Ln SW, Rochester, MN 55902-2084

Closest City or Town: Rochester, Minnesota

How to Get There: From US Highway 14, take 2nd St SW exit and head south on 14th Ave SW, then turn right onto Plummer Ln SW.

GPS Coordinates: 44.0105471° N, 92.4795974° W

Best Time to Visit: Spring through fall for garden tours and outdoor events

Pass/Permit/Fees: Free; some events may have fees.

Did You Know? The Plummer House features over 300 feet of underground tunnels.

Website:
http://www.rochestermn.gov/departments/park/facilities/plummerhouse/index.asp

Quarry Hill Nature Center

Unleash your inner explorer at Quarry Hill Nature Center in Rochester, Minnesota. This vibrant center offers a myriad of recreational activities, including hiking through diverse habitats, bird-watching, and exploring the on-site cave. The interactive exhibits and live animals provide educational fun for all ages. Nestled in a 329-acre park, visitors can also enjoy the butterfly garden and fossil hunting in the former quarry.

Location: 701 Silver Creek Rd NE, Rochester, MN 55906-4504

Closest City or Town: Rochester, Minnesota

How to Get There: From US Highway 52, take the 37th St exit east, then turn right on Silver Creek Rd NE and follow signs to the nature center.

GPS Coordinates: 44.0300157° N, 92.4302528° W

Best Time to Visit: Year-round, with seasonal activities

Pass/Permit/Fees: Free; some programs may have fees.

Did You Know? The nature center is home to over 35 species of live animals, including reptiles and birds of prey.

Website: http://www.qhnc.org/

Soldiers Field Veterans Memorial

Honor the bravery and sacrifices of military veterans at the Soldiers Field Veterans Memorial in Rochester, Minnesota. This poignant memorial park features granite walls engraved with the names of local veterans, beautifully landscaped gardens, and statues commemorating the service of all military branches. Visitors can reflect on the comprehensive history of the U.S. armed forces while strolling through this solemn and respectful space.

Location: 300 7th St SE, Rochester, MN 55904-7310

Closest City or Town: Rochester, Minnesota

How to Get There: From US Highway 63, take the 6th St SW exit and head east, then turn south onto Memorial Parkway SE and follow signs to the memorial.

GPS Coordinates: 44.0154469° N, 92.4672919° W

Best Time to Visit: Year-round

Pass/Permit/Fees: Free

Did You Know? The memorial includes a Wall of Honor listing the names of over 3,000 local veterans.

Website: http://www.soldiersfieldmemorial.org/

The Plummer Building Mayo Clinic Historical Suite

Step into history at The Plummer Building Mayo Clinic Historical Suite in Rochester, Minnesota. This iconic building is an architectural masterpiece and a symbol of medical innovation. Visitors can explore the grand Historical Suite, learn about the Mayo Clinic's pioneering work, and admire the intricate details of the building's design. Highlights include historic medical instruments and original furnishings that offer a glimpse into the past.

Location: 200 1st St SW, Rochester, MN 55905-0001

Closest City or Town: Rochester, Minnesota

How to Get There: From US Highway 63, take 2nd St SW west, and the building is located at the intersection of 1st St SW and 3rd Ave SW.

GPS Coordinates: 44.0223132° N, 92.4667642° W

Best Time to Visit: Year-round

Pass/Permit/Fees: Free

Did You Know? The Plummer Building features a carillon with 56 bells, weighing over 18 tons in total.

Website:

https://history.mayoclinic.org/tours-events/plummer-building/

SAINT PAUL

Cathedral of Saint Paul

Discover architectural grandeur and spiritual tranquility at the Cathedral of Saint Paul. This majestic structure, with its stunning stained glass windows and impressive dome, invites visitors to explore its awe-inspiring beauty. Located in the heart of Saint Paul, this cathedral stands as a testament to the city's rich history and heritage. Visitors can marvel at its intricate architectural details, attend a serene mass, or simply enjoy a moment of quiet reflection. The unique feature of this cathedral is its magnificent dome, one of the largest in the world, offering a breathtaking sight both inside and out.

Location: 239 Selby Ave, Saint Paul, MN 55102-1811

Closest City or Town: Saint Paul, Minnesota

How to Get There: From downtown Saint Paul, head west on Kellogg Blvd E, turn right onto John Ireland Blvd, and then left onto Selby Ave. The cathedral is prominently located at the intersection.

GPS Coordinates: 44.9469500° N, 93.1091430° W

Best Time to Visit: Year-round

Pass/Permit/Fees: Free

Did You Know? The cathedral's dome is 76 feet in diameter and rises 186 feet above the nave.

Website: http://www.cathedralsaintpaul.org/

Como Park Zoo & Conservatory

Immerse yourself in a world of natural beauty and wildlife at the Como Park Zoo & Conservatory in Saint Paul. This enchanting destination features a diverse array of animal exhibits, stunning botanical gardens, and engaging family-friendly activities. Visitors can stroll through the lush conservatory, meet exotic animals like gorillas and zebras, and enjoy seasonal events and programs. The conservatory's Victorian-style glass structure is a marvel, housing an array of tropical plants and flowers that bloom year-round.

Location: 1225 Estabrook Dr, Saint Paul, MN 55103-1022

Closest City or Town: Saint Paul, Minnesota

How to Get There: From downtown Saint Paul, take N Lexington Pkwy to Estabrook Dr and follow signs to the zoo and conservatory.

GPS Coordinates: 44.9812012° N, 93.1524485° W

Best Time to Visit: Spring through fall for the gardens; year-round for indoor exhibits

Pass/Permit/Fees: Free; donations appreciated

Did You Know? Como Park Zoo & Conservatory has been delighting visitors since 1897, making it one of the oldest zoos in the United States.

Website: https://comozooconservatory.org/

Fort Snelling State Park

Embark on a journey through Minnesota's natural and historical heritage at Fort Snelling State Park. Located where the Mississippi and Minnesota rivers converge, this park offers scenic hiking trails, picnic spots, and opportunities for fishing and bird-watching. Visitors can explore the park's rich history, including its significance as a military outpost. Highlights include the riverside trails and the picturesque Snelling Lake, perfect for canoeing and kayaking.

Location: 101 Snelling Lake Rd, Saint Paul, MN 55111-4116

Closest City or Town: Saint Paul, Minnesota

How to Get There: From downtown Saint Paul, head west on I-94, take exit 239B for MN-55, and follow signs to Snelling Lake Rd.

GPS Coordinates: 44.8735909° N, 93.1913828° W

Best Time to Visit: Spring through fall for outdoor activities

Pass/Permit/Fees: State park vehicle permit required

Did You Know? Fort Snelling State Park is home to Pike Island, historically significant as a meeting place for Dakota tribes.

Website:
http://www.dnr.state.mn.us/state_parks/fort_snelling/index.html

Historic Fort Snelling

Step into the past at Historic Fort Snelling, a meticulously restored military outpost perched above the Mississippi and Minnesota rivers in Saint Paul. Explore the barracks, learn about the fort's role in American history, and engage with interactive exhibits. Witness reenactments and demonstrations that bring history to life. The unique location atop a bluff offers stunning views, and the site's comprehensive educational programs make it perfect for history enthusiasts and families.

Location: 200 Tower Ave, Saint Paul, MN 55111-4037

Closest City or Town: Saint Paul, Minnesota

How to Get There: From downtown Saint Paul, take I-35E south, exit at MN-5 W, and follow signs to Historic Fort Snelling.

GPS Coordinates: 44.8927920° N, 93.1808500° W

Best Time to Visit: Spring through fall for tours and reenactments

Pass/Permit/Fees: Admission fees apply; check the website for details

Did You Know? Historic Fort Snelling has been a strategic site since the 1820s and played a key role during the U.S.-Dakota War of 1862.

Website: https://www.mnhs.org/fortsnelling

James J. Hill House

Discover the opulence of the Gilded Age at the James J. Hill House in Saint Paul. This magnificent mansion, once home to railroad magnate James J. Hill, offers an alluring glimpse into the lavish lifestyle of one of America's most influential figures. Visitors can take guided tours through the mansion's richly decorated rooms, marvel at intricate woodwork, and explore exhibits that tell the story of Hill's impact on transportation and industry. The house's grandeur and historical significance make it a captivating destination for history buffs and architecture enthusiasts.

Location: 240 Summit Ave, Saint Paul, MN 55102-2194

Closest City or Town: Saint Paul, Minnesota

How to Get There: From downtown Saint Paul, take Summit Ave west, and the house is located near the intersection with Nina St.

GPS Coordinates: 44.9450818° N, 93.1089199° W

Best Time to Visit: Year-round

Pass/Permit/Fees: Entrance fees apply; check the website for details

Did You Know? The James J. Hill House includes a 100-foot reception hall and a pipe organ with 1,006 pipes.

Website: http://www.mnhs.org/hillhouse"

Landmark Center

Discover the architectural grandeur and cultural heritage at Landmark Center, an iconic building nestled in downtown Saint Paul, Minnesota. Once a federal courthouse and post office, this magnificent structure now serves as a vibrant cultural center. Explore its beautiful Romanesque Revival architecture, take part in a variety of public exhibits, and attend live performances or historical tours. Its elegant interior, complete with stone archways and stained glass windows, provides a stunning backdrop for visitors to learn about the region's history and art.

Location: 75 5th St W, Saint Paul, MN 55102-1431

Closest City or Town: Saint Paul, Minnesota

How to Get There: Easily accessible from Interstate 94, take the 5th St exit and follow signs to Landmark Center.

GPS Coordinates: 44.9459645° N, 93.0971395° W

Best Time to Visit: Year-round, with varied events and exhibits throughout the year.

Pass/Permit/Fees: Free; some events may have fees.

Did You Know? Landmark Center was saved from demolition in the 1970s and restored to become a cultural jewel of Saint Paul.

Website: http://www.landmarkcenter.org/

Minnesota Children's Museum

Ignite creativity and imagination at the Minnesota Children's Museum, located in the heart of Saint Paul, Minnesota. This interactive museum is designed to provide hands-on learning experiences for children. Kids can climb, splash, and explore in a variety of themed exhibits that stimulate curiosity and discovery. Whether navigating the whimsical Habitot for toddlers or delving into the interactive The Scramble, there's something for every young explorer.

Location: 10 7th St W, Saint Paul, MN 55102-1104

Closest City or Town: Saint Paul, Minnesota

How to Get There: Situated downtown, accessible via Interstate 94, take the 10th St exit and follow signs to the museum.

GPS Coordinates: 44.9475994° N, 93.0970363° W

Best Time to Visit: Year-round, with seasonal exhibits adding new excitement.

Pass/Permit/Fees: Admission fees apply; check website for current rates.

Did You Know? The museum underwent a major expansion in 2017, doubling its size and adding new attractions.

Website: https://mcm.org/

Minnesota History Center

Immerse yourself in Minnesota's rich past at the Minnesota History Center, a dynamic museum located in Saint Paul. Discover engaging exhibits that cover a wide range of topics, from the state's natural history to its industrial rise. Interactive displays, historical artifacts, and storytelling bring the region's storied past to life. Notable features include a 24-ton boxcar and multimedia exhibits that transport you through time.

Location: 345 Kellogg Blvd W, Saint Paul, MN 55102-1903

Closest City or Town: Saint Paul, Minnesota

How to Get There: Easily reachable from Interstate 94, take the 10th St exit and head west on Kellogg Blvd.

GPS Coordinates: 44.9495556° N, 93.1055520° W

Best Time to Visit: Year-round

Pass/Permit/Fees: Admission fees apply; see website for details.

Did You Know? The center also houses the Gale Family Library, a treasure trove for researchers and genealogists.

Website: http://www.mnhs.org/historycenter

Minnesota State Capitol

Explore the majestic Minnesota State Capitol, a Beaux-Arts masterpiece located in Saint Paul. Designed by renowned architect Cass Gilbert, this stunning capitol building features an impressive marble dome and intricate frescoes. Visitors can take guided tours to learn about Minnesota's legislative process, architectural history, and civic art. Inside, discover breathtaking rotundas, chambers, and works of art that reflect the state's heritage.

Location: 75 Rev Dr Martin Luther King Jr Blvd, Saint Paul, MN 55155-1605

Closest City or Town: Saint Paul, Minnesota

How to Get There: From Interstate 94, take the 12th St exit and head north on Reverend Dr. Martin Luther King Jr Blvd.

GPS Coordinates: 44.9552186° N, 93.1022446° W

Best Time to Visit: Year-round, with holiday events adding special charm.

Pass/Permit/Fees: Free; guided tour fees may apply.

Did You Know? The Capitol's limestone structure is crowned with a dome that ranks among the largest self-supported marble domes in the world.

Website: http://www.mnhs.org/capitol

Minnesota State Fair

Indulge in a cornucopia of entertainment at the Minnesota State Fair, held annually in Saint Paul. Known as the Great Minnesota Get-Together, the fair showcases agricultural exhibits, thrilling rides, live concerts, and an array of food that's deep-fried and on a stick. Spanning 12 days, this is Minnesota's most celebrated event, drawing millions of visitors each year.

Location: 1265 Snelling Ave N, Saint Paul, MN 55108-3003

Closest City or Town: Saint Paul, Minnesota

How to Get There: Accessible from Interstate 94, take the Snelling Ave exit north, and follow signs to the fairgrounds.

GPS Coordinates: 44.9811287° N, 93.1676283° W

Best Time to Visit: Late August to early September

Pass/Permit/Fees: Admission fees apply; check website for prices.

Did You Know? The Minnesota State Fair offers over 500 different food items, including the iconic Pronto Pup corn dog.

Website: http://www.mnstatefair.org/

Science Museum of Minnesota

Find your sense of wonder and discovery at the Science Museum of Minnesota, a premier destination for interactive exhibits and scientific exploration in Saint Paul. Dive into the world of dinosaurs, participate in hands-on experiments, and explore the mysteries of the universe in their state-of-the-art Omnitheater. Located along the Mississippi River, this museum provides an engaging experience for visitors of all ages, sparking curiosity and excitement.

Location: 120 Kellogg Blvd W, Saint Paul, MN 55102-1202

Closest City or Town: Saint Paul, Minnesota

How to Get There: Easily accessible from I-94, take the Kellogg Blvd exit, and the museum is located along the river.

GPS Coordinates: 44.9424870° N, 93.0987980° W

Best Time to Visit: Year-round, with special exhibits during school breaks and holidays

Pass/Permit/Fees: Varies by exhibit; see website for details.

Did You Know? The museum houses over 1.75 million artifacts and specimens.

Website: http://www.smm.org/

Xcel Energy Center

Feel the excitement of world-class events and concerts at the Xcel Energy Center, home to the NHL's Minnesota Wild in Saint Paul. This versatile arena hosts thrilling hockey games, star-studded concerts, and dynamic shows, offering exceptional entertainment experiences. Located in the vibrant downtown area, visitors can easily enjoy nearby restaurants and nightlife before or after events.

Location: 199 Kellogg Blvd W, Saint Paul, MN 55102-1200

Closest City or Town: Saint Paul, Minnesota

How to Get There: Accessible from I-94, take the 5th St exit, and follow signs to the arena.

GPS Coordinates: 44.9448133° N, 93.1011174° W

Best Time to Visit: Year-round, with peak activities during hockey season and major concert tours

Pass/Permit/Fees: Ticket prices vary; check the website for event details.

Did You Know? The Xcel Energy Center can transform from an ice rink to a concert hall in just hours.

Website: http://www.saintpaularena.com/

SCHROEDER

Temperance River State Park

Revel in the natural beauty and rugged charm of Temperance River State Park, nestled along Minnesota's North Shore in Schroeder. This park offers exceptional hiking trails, cascading waterfalls, and panoramic vistas of Lake Superior. Experience the unique geology of the Temperance River Gorge, or enjoy camping under the starry skies.

Location: 7620 West Hwy 61, Schroeder, MN 55613

Closest City or Town: Schroeder, Minnesota

How to Get There: Take MN-61 N from Duluth, continue for about 80 miles and the park entrance is well-marked.

GPS Coordinates: 47.5557014° N, 90.8718553° W

Best Time to Visit: Late spring to early fall for hiking and camping; winter for snowshoeing.

Pass/Permit/Fees: State park vehicle permit required.

Did You Know? Unlike most rivers, the Temperance River has no sandbars.

Website:
http://www.dnr.state.mn.us/state_parks/temperance_river/index.ht ml

SHAKOPEE

Valleyfair

Unleash your thrill-seeking spirit at Valleyfair, the largest amusement park in Minnesota, located in Shakopee. With over 75 rides and attractions, including high-speed roller coasters, a water park, and family-friendly rides, there's something for everyone. Nestled along the Minnesota River, this park offers endless excitement for a perfect day of fun.

Location: 1 Valleyfair Dr, Shakopee, MN 55379-3098

Closest City or Town: Shakopee, Minnesota

How to Get There: Easily accessible via US-169 S, take the Valleyfair Dr exit and follow signs to the entrance.

GPS Coordinates: 44.8004134° N, 93.4564059° W

Best Time to Visit: Late spring through early fall.

Pass/Permit/Fees: Admission fees vary; check the website for current pricing.

Did You Know? Valleyfair covers over 125 acres, making it one of the largest amusement parks in the Midwest.

Website: http://www.valleyfair.com/

SHEVLIN

Mississippi Headwaters

Discover the birthplace of America's great river at Mississippi Headwaters, located in Itasca State Park in northern Minnesota. This historic site marks the beginning of the mighty Mississippi River as it flows out from Lake Itasca. Visitors can walk across the gentle stream, hike through ancient forests, and enjoy the tranquility of this natural landmark. This unique destination offers a blend of scenic beauty and historical significance.

Location: 6QRQ+3H Shevlin, Minnesota

Closest City or Town: Shevlin, Minnesota

How to Get There: From U.S. Highway 71, enter Itasca State Park and follow signs to the headwaters.

GPS Coordinates: 47.2401875° N, 95.2110625° W

Best Time to Visit: Summer for the best weather; fall for beautiful foliage.

Pass/Permit/Fees: State park vehicle permit required.

Did You Know? The Mississippi River is the second-longest river in North America, flowing over 2,300 miles to the Gulf of Mexico.

Website: http://www.dnr.state.mn.us/state_parks/Itasca/index.html

SILVER BAY

High Falls

Discover the beauty and power of the High Falls at Tettegouche State Park. Nestled in Silver Bay, this majestic waterfall cascades over 60 feet, offering a stunning spectacle against the rugged backdrop of lush forests. Visitors can hike the scenic trails, admire the falls from multiple viewpoints, and enjoy picnicking by the tranquil waters. The unique feature of High Falls is its dramatic plunge, creating misty vistas that captivate photographers and nature enthusiasts alike.

Location: Tettegouche State Park, 5702 MN-61, Silver Bay, MN 55614

Closest City or Town: Silver Bay, Minnesota

How to Get There: From Silver Bay, take MN-61 North for about 4 miles. The park entrance is well-marked.

GPS Coordinates: 47.3393554° N, 91.1959925° W

Best Time to Visit: Spring through fall

Pass/Permit/Fees: State park vehicle permit required

Did You Know? The High Falls is the highest waterfall fully within Minnesota's state boundaries.

Website:
http://www.gowaterfalling.com/waterfalls/pigeonhigh.shtml

Tettegouche State Park

Dive into the diverse landscapes of Tettegouche State Park, where adventure awaits in Silver Bay, Minnesota. Wander through rugged cliffs, dense forests, and serene lakes, offering excellent hiking, rock climbing, and bird-watching opportunities. Canoe on Baptism River, fish in Lake Superior, or simply soak up the panoramic views. Unique features include the dramatic Palisade Head cliff and the serene Shovel Point overlook, providing breathtaking vistas and tranquil spots for reflection.

Location: 5702 Highway 61 Silver Bay, MN 55614

Closest City or Town: Silver Bay, Minnesota

How to Get There: Take MN-61 North from Silver Bay for about 4 miles; the park entrance is well-marked.

GPS Coordinates: 47.3393554° N, 91.1959925° W

Best Time to Visit: Spring through fall

Pass/Permit/Fees: State park vehicle permit required

Did You Know? Tettegouche State Park is known for its diverse ecosystems, from cliffs and lakes to waterfalls and forests.

Website:
http://www.dnr.state.mn.us/state_parks/tettegouche/index.html

SOUDAN

Soudan Underground Mine

Venture into the depths of Minnesota's mining history at the Soudan Underground Mine. Located in Soudan, this former iron ore mine offers a unique underground tour, taking visitors 2,341 feet below the surface. Learn about the mining process, participate in educational programs, and experience the eerie yet fascinating world beneath the earth. Highlights include the original mine shafts and a ride on the mine's cage elevator that adds a thrill to the educational journey.

Location: 1302 McKinley Park Rd, Soudan, MN 55782

Closest City or Town: Soudan, Minnesota

How to Get There: From downtown Soudan, take McKinley Park Rd (County Road 707) for about 1 mile.

GPS Coordinates: 47.8194422° N, 92.2419835° W

Best Time to Visit: Summer and fall

Pass/Permit/Fees: Admission fees apply; check the website for details.

Did You Know? The Soudan Mine is known as Minnesota's first iron ore mine, operational since 1882.

Website:
https://www.dnr.state.mn.us/state_parks/park.html?id=spk00285#homepage

St Cloud

Clemens Gardens

Step into a world of floral beauty at Clemens Gardens in St Cloud, Minnesota. These meticulously designed gardens feature an array of colorful blooms, elegant fountains, and artistic sculptures, providing a serene escape for visitors. Wander through themed areas like the Rose Garden and the Perennial Garden, each offering unique horticultural displays and scenic pathways perfect for leisurely strolls.

Location: 1301 Kilian Blvd SE #56301, St Cloud, MN 56304

Closest City or Town: St Cloud, Minnesota

How to Get There: From downtown St Cloud, follow Riverside Dr SE south, then turn left on Kilian Blvd.

GPS Coordinates: 45.5512809° N, 94.1430993° W

Best Time to Visit: Spring through fall

Pass/Permit/Fees: Free

Did You Know? Clemens Gardens were established in 1990 and feature over 1,100 rose bushes.

Website: https://www.munsingerclemens.com/

Munsinger Gardens

Discover a botanical paradise at Munsinger Gardens in St Cloud, Minnesota. Situated along the scenic Mississippi River, these gardens offer lush greenery, vibrant floral beds, and tranquil walking paths. Enjoy the fragrance of roses, explore the whimsical sculptures, and relax by the peaceful fountains. Unique attractions include the playful peacock statues and the charming gift shop housed in a historic greenhouse.

Location: 1302 Riverside Dr SE, St Cloud, MN 56304

Closest City or Town: St Cloud, Minnesota

How to Get There: From downtown St Cloud, head south on Riverside Dr SE; the gardens are just past the Clemens Gardens.

GPS Coordinates: 45.5514024° N, 94.1445174° W

Best Time to Visit: Spring through fall

Pass/Permit/Fees: Free

Did You Know? Munsinger Gardens were established in the 1930s and include several historical structures from the Works Progress Administration era.

Website: http://ci.stcloud.mn.us/161/Munsinger-Clemens-Gardens

St Paul

Grand Avenue

Discover the charm of Grand Avenue, a bustling thoroughfare in St. Paul filled with unique shops, delectable eateries, and historic architecture. Find your sense of adventure by exploring its vibrant mix of local boutiques, cafes, and restaurants, each offering a taste of the community's rich cultural tapestry. Located in the heart of St. Paul, this avenue is not just a shopping destination but a lively hub where visitors can enjoy special events, historic homes, and a warm neighborhood vibe.

Location: 1261 Grand Ave, St Paul, MN 55105

Closest City or Town: St. Paul, Minnesota

How to Get There: From downtown St. Paul, take Summit Ave south and turn right on Victoria St, then left onto Grand Ave.

GPS Coordinates: 44.9403880° N, 93.1533118° W

Best Time to Visit: Year-round, with special events in summer and winter

Pass/Permit/Fees: Free

Did You Know? Grand Avenue is home to several historic mansions and buildings from the late 19th to early 20th century.

Website: http://www.grandave.com/

Summit Avenue

Walk through history along Summit Avenue, a picturesque street in St. Paul renowned for its grand Victorian mansions and tree-lined elegance. Embark on a leisurely stroll or bike ride to admire the well-preserved architecture of historic homes, many of which date back to the 1800s. Known for its serene beauty, Summit Avenue offers a glimpse into the city's affluent past while providing a tranquil escape from modern-day hustle and bustle.

Location: 235 Summit Ave, St Paul, MN 55102

Closest City or Town: St. Paul, Minnesota

How to Get There: From downtown St. Paul, head west on Summit Ave, starting near the Cathedral of Saint Paul.

GPS Coordinates: 44.9459762° N, 93.1094455° W

Best Time to Visit: Spring through fall for the lush foliage and warm weather

Pass/Permit/Fees: Free

Did You Know? Summit Avenue has the longest stretch of virtually uninterrupted Victorian architecture in the United States.

Website: http://sites.mnhs.org/historic-sites/james-j-hill-house/summit-avenue-walking-tour

STILLWATER

Stillwater Lift Bridge

Discover the engineering marvel of the Stillwater Lift Bridge, an iconic landmark linking Minnesota and Wisconsin over the St. Croix River. Originally built in 1931, this historic lift bridge is still operational, allowing boats to pass by raising its central span. Visitors can enjoy scenic river views, indulge in a leisurely stroll across the bridge, and explore the charming town of Stillwater with its riverside shops and eateries.

Location: 106 Chestnut St E, Stillwater, MN 55082-5116

Closest City or Town: Stillwater, Minnesota

How to Get There: From Highway 36, take the exit for Stillwater Blvd N and head east on Chestnut St E.

GPS Coordinates: 45.0563130° N, 92.8035850° W

Best Time to Visit: Spring through fall for the best weather and boat activity

Pass/Permit/Fees: Free

Did You Know? The Stillwater Lift Bridge was placed on the National Register of Historic Places in 1989.

Website: http://www.dot.state.mn.us/metro/projects/liftbridge

Teddy Bear Park

Bring the family to Teddy Bear Park in Stillwater, a whimsical playground designed for young children. This charming park features teddy bear-themed play structures, picnic areas, and beautifully landscaped gardens. Children can climb, slide, and explore the imaginative play zones, making it an ideal spot for a fun-filled day outdoors.

Location: South 2nd Street and Nelson Street, Stillwater, MN 55082

Closest City or Town: Stillwater, Minnesota

How to Get There: From downtown Stillwater, drive south on Main St S and turn right onto 2nd St S.

GPS Coordinates: 45.0537990° N, 92.8059650° W

Best Time to Visit: Late spring through early fall for the best weather

Pass/Permit/Fees: Free

Did You Know? Teddy Bear Park was designed with input from local children, making it a community-driven project.

Website:

https://secure.rec1.com/MN/stillwater-mn/catalog/index?filter=bG9jYXRpb24lNUIzMzEwMSU1RD0xJnNlYXJjaD0mcmVudGFsJTVCZnJvbSU1RD0mcmVudGFsJTVCdG8lNUQ9

TAYLORS FALLS

Interstate State Park

Find your sense of adventure at Interstate State Park, located along the scenic St. Croix River in Taylors Falls. This park offers a plethora of outdoor activities, from hiking and rock climbing to canoeing and fishing. Explore the glacial potholes formed over 10,000 years ago, marvel at the unique rock formations, or enjoy a serene boat ride on the river. Known for its natural beauty and geological wonders, Interstate State Park is a haven for both thrill-seekers and nature lovers.

Location: 307 Milltown Road, Taylors Falls, MN 55084

Closest City or Town: Taylors Falls, Minnesota

How to Get There: Take Highway 95 (St. Croix Trail) north to Milltown Road in Taylors Falls and turn right into the park entrance.

GPS Coordinates: 45.3936675° N, 92.6689911° W

Best Time to Visit: Spring through fall for ideal hiking conditions; winter for cross-country skiing

Pass/Permit/Fees: State park vehicle permit required

Did You Know? Interstate State Park is home to some of the world's deepest glacial potholes, with some measuring over 60 feet deep.

Website:
https://www.dnr.state.mn.us/state_parks/interstate/index.html

TWO HARBORS

Gooseberry Falls State Park

Unleash your adventurous spirit at Gooseberry Falls State Park, a haven for outdoor enthusiasts located along Minnesota's North Shore in Two Harbors. Immerse yourself in the park's breathtaking natural beauty, featuring glorious waterfalls, scenic vistas, and rugged lakeshore. Wander through miles of hiking trails, marvel at the cascading falls, and explore the diverse flora and fauna along the way. This park's unique charm lies in its picturesque waterfalls, making it a perfect destination for scenic photography and nature walks.

Location: 3206 Highway 61 East, Two Harbors, MN 55616

Closest City or Town: Two Harbors, Minnesota

How to Get There: From Two Harbors, take MN-61 N for about 13 miles, and the park entrance will be on the right.

GPS Coordinates: 47.1396330° N, 91.4731362° W

Best Time to Visit: Spring through fall for hiking and waterfall views

Pass/Permit/Fees: State park vehicle permit required

Did You Know? Gooseberry Falls is often called the "Gateway to the North Shore" due to its stunning landscapes and welcoming atmosphere.

Website:
http://www.dnr.state.mn.us/state_parks/gooseberry_falls/index.html

Split Rock Lighthouse

Set your sights on the iconic Split Rock Lighthouse, majestically perched on a towering cliff overlooking Lake Superior in Two Harbors, Minnesota. This historical lighthouse, now a museum, offers visitors a glimpse into maritime history with fascinating tours and exhibits. Experience the awe-inspiring views from the observation deck, or delve into the tales of shipwrecks that prompted the lighthouse's construction. This landmark's unique feature is its breathtaking backdrop, offering unparalleled views of Lake Superior's rugged coastline.

Location: 3713 Split Rock Lighthouse Rd., Two Harbors, MN 55616-2020

Closest City or Town: Two Harbors, Minnesota

How to Get There: Travel north on MN-61 from Two Harbors for about 20 miles, then turn right onto Split Rock Lighthouse Rd and follow signs to the lighthouse.

GPS Coordinates: 47.2039530° N, 91.3683157° W

Best Time to Visit: Spring through fall for the best weather and visibility

Pass/Permit/Fees: Admission fees apply for lighthouse tours

Did You Know? Split Rock Lighthouse was completed in 1910 and is one of the most photographed lighthouses in the United States.

Website: http://www.mnhs.org/splitrock

Split Rock Lighthouse State Park

Find your perfect outdoor escape at Split Rock Lighthouse State Park, nestled on the scenic North Shore of Lake Superior in Two Harbors. This park offers a variety of recreational activities, including hiking, fishing, and camping, all set against the backdrop of the historic Split Rock Lighthouse. Explore rugged trails, enjoy a picnic on the shoreline, or kayak along the rocky coastlines. The park's unique draw is its stunning lighthouse view, making it a picturesque setting for outdoor enthusiasts.

Location: 3755 Split Rock Lighthouse Rd, Two Harbors, MN 55616-2020

Closest City or Town: Two Harbors, Minnesota

How to Get There: Head north on MN-61 from Two Harbors for approximately 19 miles, then follow signs to Split Rock Lighthouse State Park.

GPS Coordinates: 47.1931329° N, 91.3942065° W

Best Time to Visit: Summer for hiking and picnicking; fall for vibrant foliage

Pass/Permit/Fees: State park vehicle permit required

Did You Know? The park includes several miles of trails with expansive views of Lake Superior and the lighthouse.

Website:
http://www.dnr.state.mn.us/state_parks/split_rock_lighthouse/index.html

Two Harbors Lighthouse

Step into maritime history at the Two Harbors Lighthouse, the oldest continuously operating lighthouse in Minnesota, located on the scenic shores of Lake Superior's Agate Bay. This historic site offers guided tours, panoramic views, and a quaint bed and breakfast within the lighthouse keeper's quarters. Wander through the museum, explore the original Fresnel lens, and enjoy the scenic trails that surround the lighthouse. The unique feature of this lighthouse is its operational status, providing a glimpse into the days of active seafaring life.

Location: Lake Superior's Agate Bay One Lighthouse Point at S end of 3rd street, Two Harbors, MN 55616

Closest City or Town: Two Harbors, Minnesota

How to Get There: Take Waterfront Dr south from downtown Two Harbors, then head east on 3rd St to the lighthouse.

GPS Coordinates: 47.0227111° N, 91.6707322° W

Best Time to Visit: Summer for the best weather and full access to the site

Pass/Permit/Fees: Admission fees apply for tours and museum entry

Did You Know? The Two Harbors Lighthouse has guided mariners since its construction in 1892.

Website: http://lakecountyhistoricalsociety.org/museums/view/two-harbors-light-station

WABASHA

National Eagle Center

Find your sense of awe and wonder at the National Eagle Center in Wabasha, Minnesota. Nestled along the banks of the Mississippi River, this incredible center offers an up-close and personal view of America's majestic bald eagles. Visitors can engage in interactive exhibits, participate in live eagle programs, and watch wild eagles soaring from the observation deck. The center is dedicated to education and conservation, making it a captivating experience for all ages to learn about these magnificent birds in their natural habitat.

Location: 50 Pembroke Ave S, Wabasha, MN 55981-1241

Closest City or Town: Wabasha, Minnesota

How to Get There: From US Highway 61, take Pembroke Ave S towards the riverfront.

GPS Coordinates: 44.3841389° N, 92.0312917° W

Best Time to Visit: Year-round, especially during winter months when eagles are most active

Pass/Permit/Fees: Admission fees apply; check the website for details.

Did You Know? The National Eagle Center offers unique educational programs such as Eagle Viewing Field Trips, which guide visitors to the best local spots for eagle watching.

Website: http://www.nationaleaglecenter.org/

WALNUT GROVE

Laura Ingalls Wilder Museum

Step into the world of a beloved American author at the Laura Ingalls Wilder Museum in Walnut Grove, Minnesota. This museum offers a fascinating glimpse into the life and legacy of Laura Ingalls Wilder, famed for her Little House on the Prairie books. Explore historical exhibits, original artifacts, and engaging displays that bring her stories to life. Located in the heart of Walnut Grove, visitors can experience the rich history and charm of this iconic literary landmark.

Location: 330 8th St, Walnut Grove, MN 56180-1114

Closest City or Town: Walnut Grove, Minnesota

How to Get There: From State Highway 14, take the Walnut Grove exit and follow signs to the museum.

GPS Coordinates: 44.2241547° N, 95.4721994° W

Best Time to Visit: Summer for the annual Laura Ingalls Wilder Pageant

Pass/Permit/Fees: Admission fees apply; see the website for current rates.

Did You Know? The museum hosts an annual Laura Ingalls Wilder Pageant, a live outdoor performance based on her books.

Website: http://www.walnutgrove.org/museum/

WINONA

Garvin Heights City Park

Soak in breathtaking panoramic views at Garvin Heights City Park in Winona, Minnesota. Perched high above the Mississippi River Valley, this park offers sweeping vistas that are perfect for photography, picnicking, or a peaceful moment of reflection. Visitors can hike up the bluff to enjoy the scenic overlooks or take a leisurely drive to the top for an unforgettable sight of the river and surrounding landscapes.

Location: 200 Garvin Heights Rd, Winona, MN 55987

Closest City or Town: Winona, Minnesota

How to Get There: From US Highway 14, follow signs to Garvin Heights Road and continue to the park entrance.

GPS Coordinates: 44.0334200° N, 91.6515370° W

Best Time to Visit: Spring through fall for clear views and comfortable weather

Pass/Permit/Fees: Free

Did You Know? Garvin Heights City Park is named after Ebenezer and Mary Garvin, early settlers of Winona who donated the land.

Website: https://en.wikipedia.org/wiki/Winona,_Minnesota

Minnesota Marine Art Museum

Embark on a voyage of artistic discovery at the Minnesota Marine Art Museum in Winona. This renowned museum showcases a stunning collection of marine artworks, including pieces by famous artists such as Van Gogh, Monet, and Picasso. Located along the picturesque Mississippi River, visitors can immerse themselves in maritime history and culture through engaging exhibits and beautiful paintings. The museum's unique location and impressive collection make it a must-visit for art enthusiasts.

Location: 800 Riverview Dr, Winona, MN 55987-2272

Closest City or Town: Winona, Minnesota

How to Get There: From US Highway 61, turn onto Riverview Drive and follow signs to the museum.

GPS Coordinates: 44.0596412° N, 91.6575720° W

Best Time to Visit: Year-round, with seasonal exhibits adding new dimensions

Pass/Permit/Fees: Admission fees apply; check the website for details.

Did You Know? The museum's collection includes works by Hudson River School painters and contemporary artists inspired by water themes.

Website: https://mmam.org/

MAP

We have devised an interactive map that includes all destinations described in the book.

Upon scanning a provided QR code, a link will be sent to your email, allowing you access to this unique digital feature.

This map is both detailed and user-friendly, marking every location described within the pages of the book. It provides accurate addresses and GPS coordinates for each location, coupled with direct links to the websites of these stunning destinations.

Once you receive your email link and access the interactive map, you'll have an immediate and comprehensive overview of each site's location. This invaluable tool simplifies trip planning and navigation, making it a crucial asset for both first-time visitors and seasoned explorers of Washington.

Scan the following QR or type in the provided link to receive it:

https://jo.my/minnesotabucketlistbonus

You will receive an email with links to access the Interactive Map. If you do not see our email, please look for it in spam or another section of your inbox.

In case you have any problems, you can write us at
TravelBucketList@becrepress.com

Made in United States
Troutdale, OR
11/24/2024

25243981R00064